LEARNING ADVENTURES IN U.S. TRAVELS
Grades 3–4

By the Staff of Score@Kaplan

Foreword by Alan Tripp

Simon & Schuster

**This series is dedicated to our
Score@Kaplan parents and children—
thank you for making these books possible.**

Published by
Kaplan Educational Centers and Simon & Schuster
1230 Avenue of the Americas
New York, NY 10020

Copyright © 1998 by Kaplan Educational Centers

All rights reserved. No part of this book may be reproduced or transmitted in any form or by any means, electronic or mechanical, including photocopying, recording, or by any information storage and retrieval system, without the written permission of the Publisher, except where permitted by law.

Kaplan is a registered trademark of Kaplan Educational Centers.

Special thanks to: Elissa Grayer, Doreen Beauregard, Julie Schmidt, Rebecca Geller Schwartz, Linda Lott, Janet Cassidy, Marlene Greil, Nancy McDonald, Sarah Jane Bryan, Chris Wilsdon, Janet Montal, Jeannette Sanderson, David Stienecker, Dan Greenberg, Kathy Wilmore, Dorrie Berkowitz, Brent Gallenberger, and Molly Walsh

Head Coach and General Manager, Score@Kaplan: Alan Tripp
President, Score@Kaplan: Robert L. Waldron
Series Content and Development: Mega-Books
Project Editor: Mary Pearce
Production Editor: Donna Mackay, Graphic Circle Inc.
Art Director: Elana Goren-Totino
Illustrators: Rick Brown, Ryan Brown, Sandy Forrest, Larry Nolte, Evan Polenghi, Fred Schrier, Peter Spacek, Arnie Ten
Cover Design: Cheung Tai
Cover Photograph: Michael Britto

Manufactured in the United States of America
Published Simultaneously in Canada

January 1998
10 9 8 7 6 5 4 3 2 1

ISBN: 0-684-84433-8

Contents

Note to Parents.. iv
Note to Kids... vi

Worldly Wise... 1
  Skills covered include graphing, written expression, studying, problem solving, observation, mapping, phonics and spelling, reading comprehension, life science, vocabulary development, and computation

The Wild West... 17
  Skills covered include fractions and decimals, computation, vocabulary, reading comprehension, grammar and usage, written expression, mapping, phonics and spelling, and studying

These Great States.. 31
  Skills covered include earth science, problem solving, graphing, phonics and spelling, vocabulary, life science, numeration, written expression, fractions and decimals, and computation

Here, There, Everywhere..................................... 46
  Skills covered include study skills, earth science, phonics and spelling, reading comprehension strategies, written expression, technology, familiarity with money, geometry, time telling, and understanding of literature

Sightseeing and Souvenirs................................... 55
  Skills covered include observation, problem solving, life science, graphing, written expression, vocabulary, mechanics, and familiarity with money

Puzzle.. 64
Answers... 65
How Do You Foster Your Child's Interest in Learning?............ 71

Dear Parents,

Your child's success in school is important to you, and at Score@Kaplan we are always pleased when the kids who attend our educational centers do well on their report cards. But what we really want for our kids is not just good grades. We also want everything that good grades are supposed to represent:

- We want our kids to master the key communication systems that make civilization possible: language (spoken and written), math, the visual arts, and music.
- We want them to build their critical-thinking skills so they can understand, appreciate, and improve their world.
- We want them to continually increase their knowledge and to value learning as the key to a happy, successful life.
- We want them to always do their best, to persist when challenged, to be a force for good, and to help others whenever they can.

These are ambitious goals, but our children deserve no less. We at Score@Kaplan have already helped thousands of children across the country in our centers, and we hope this series of books for children in first through sixth grades will reach many more households.

Simple Principles

We owe the remarkable success of Score@Kaplan to a few simple principles. This book was developed with these principles in mind.

- We expect every child to succeed.
- We make it possible for every child to succeed.
- We reinforce every instance of success, no matter how small.

Assessing Your Child

One helpful approach in assessing your child's skills is to ask yourself the following questions.

- How much is my child reading? At what level of difficulty?
- Has my child mastered appropriate language arts skills, such as spelling, grammar, and syntax?
- Does my child have the ability to express appropriately complex thoughts when speaking or writing?
- Does my child demonstrate mastery of all age-appropriate math skills, such as mastery of addition and subtraction facts, multiplication tables, division rules, and so on?

These questions are a good starting place and may give you new insights into your child's academic situation.

What's Going on at School

Parents will always need to monitor the situation at school and take responsibility for their child's learning. You should find out what your child should be learning at each grade level and match that against what your child actually learns.

The activity pages in *Learning Adventures* were developed using the standards developed by the professional teachers associations. As your child explores the activities in *Learning Adventures*, you might find that a particular concept hasn't been taught in school or hasn't yet been mastered by your child. This presents a great opportunity for both of you. Together you can learn something new.

Encouraging Your Child to Learn at Home

This book is full of fun learning activities you can do with your child to build understanding of key concepts in language arts, math, and science. Most activities are designed for your child to do independently. But that doesn't mean that you can't work on them together or invite your child to share the work with you. As you help your child learn, please bear in mind the following observations drawn from experience in our centers:

- Positive reinforcement is the key. Try to maintain a ratio of at least five positive remarks to every negative one.
- All praise must be genuine. Try praises such as: "That was a good try," "You got this part of it right," or "I'm proud of you for doing your best, even though it was hard."
- When a child gets stuck, giving the answer is often not the most efficient way to help. Ask open-ended questions, or rephrase the problem.
- Remember to be patient and supportive. Children need to learn that hard work pays off.

There's More to Life Than Academic Learning

Most parents recognize that academic excellence is just one of the many things they would like to ensure for their children. At Score@Kaplan, we are committed to developing the whole child. These books are designed to emphasize academic skills and critical thinking, as well as provide an opportunity for positive reinforcement and encouragement from you, the parent.

We wish you a successful and rewarding experience as you and your child embark upon this learning adventure together.

Alan Tripp
General Manager
Score@Kaplan

Dear Kids,

Get your pencils sharpened, and put your game face on! You're about to start a Learning Adventure. This book is filled with puzzles, games, riddles and lots of other fun stuff. You can do them alone or with your family and friends. While you're at it, you'll exercise your brain.

If you get stuck on something, look for the Score coaches. Think of them as your personal brain trainers. You can also check your answers on pages 65–70, if you really have to.

We know you will do a great job. That's why we have a special puzzle inside. After you do three or four pages, you'll see a puzzle piece. Cut it out, then glue it or tape it in place on page 64. When you're done with the book, the puzzle will be done, too. Then you'll find a secret message from us.

So, pump up your mind muscles and get ready to Score. You'll have a blast and boost your brain power at the same time.

Go for it!

Your Coaches at Score

NAME_____

Worldly Wise
Read bar graphs

Where in the World?

Gloria Globetrotter is excited about taking a vacation. She wants to visit a place where the weather is mild. She's decided to do a little research before making any definite plans. Look carefully at Gloria's requirements. Then read the graphs. Use the information to answer the question below.

Be sure to look only at the month in which Gloria will need to travel. If it is hard for you to tell exactly how tall a bar is, use a ruler to draw a straight line across the graph from the top of the bar to the appropriate number.

Gloria's Requirements:

- She will be traveling in March.
- She wants to go someplace where it won't be cooler than 0 degrees Celsius. (This is the temperature at which water freezes.)
- She wants to go someplace where it won't be warmer than 30 degrees Celsius. (This is a temperature that makes you want to jump into a swimming pool.)

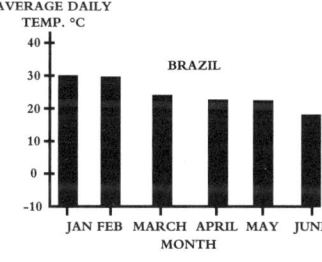
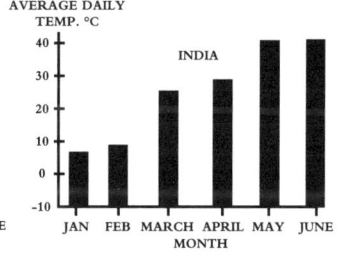
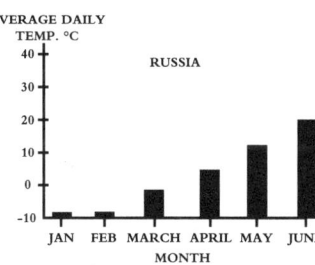
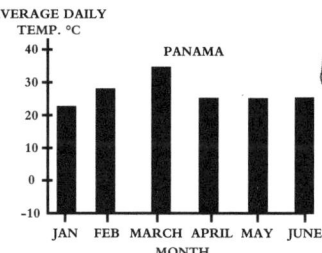

Which two countries would Gloria probably enjoy visiting? _____

_____

Grades 3 & 4

1

Worldly Wise
Write to persuade

NAME _____

Make a Brochure

A travel brochure tells all about a place and makes it sound like a great place to visit. Try making a travel brochure about your own state. Use the questions below to help you get started. Then use another sheet of paper to make the brochure.

To make your brochure, fold a piece of paper so that it has 3 sections. Draw an exciting picture on the front and include the name of your state. Put other information inside. Be sure to include lots of pictures!

1. What are some important events that take place in your state, such as festivals, fairs, or sporting events? _____
_____
_____

2. What are some beautiful places to visit in your state? _____
_____
_____

3. What amusement parks, recreation areas, or other activities for kids are found in your state? _____
_____
_____

4. What unusual or historic buildings are in your state? _____
_____

5. What kinds of museums and parks are in your state? _____
_____

6. What can people see or do in your state that they can't do anywhere else? _____
_____

Around the House: Ask a parent or sibling to help you get brochures from other cities, towns, and states. (You can get them by writing or calling a state tourist board or local chamber of commerce.) Which ones make you want to visit the places they advertise? Why do they make you feel that way?

Grades 3 & 4

Worldly Wise
Alphabetize words

NAME_____

Don't Forget Your Socks!

Before you leave on a trip, it's a good idea to make a checklist of the things you want to bring. Then you can simply check them off as you pack. Here's a checklist of items Owen Overpacker is planning to take on his beach vacation. Put the items in alphabetical order on the lines. We did the first one for you to help you get started.

Remember, if two words start with the same letter, you'll have to compare their second letters. And if those letters are the same, you'll have to move to the third letters. (And sometimes even the fourth, fifth, sixth, etc.!)

Owen's Packing List

beach bucket	inflatable shark
shovel	sandals
beach towel	sandwiches
sunscreen	juice
umbrella	boat
~~bathing suit~~	jeans
shorts	sweater
shirts	cap
sunglasses	sneakers
beach ball	socks

bathing suit
_____
_____
_____
_____

_____
_____
_____
_____
_____
_____
_____
_____
_____
_____

Around the House: Work with your parents to make a grocery list of all the items your family usually needs. Put it in alphabetical order. Make many copies of the sheet. When your parents go shopping, they can check off the items they need.

Grades 3 & 4

Worldly Wise
Calculate with measurement

NAME _____

Weight in Line

Clyde Clutter is packing for his trip, but he knows that he can't bring everything he wants. He's flying on a small plane, and the contents of the suitcase he brings aboard may weigh only 35 pounds. Use the weights marked on each of these objects to decide which 10 things Clyde can bring with him. After checking your math carefully, circle the 10 items you have selected.

Good job—that activity is in the bag! Now put this puzzle piece in the frame on page 64. Cut it out, then glue or tape it in place!

- 9 lbs.
- 2 lbs.
- 6 lbs.
- 4 lbs.
- 7 lbs.
- 4 lbs.
- 2 lbs.
- $1\frac{1}{2}$ lbs.
- 1 lb.
- $\frac{1}{2}$ lb.
- 5 lbs.
- 3 lbs.
- 1 lb.
- $2\frac{1}{2}$ lbs.
- $5\frac{1}{2}$ lbs.
- 10 lbs.

Think About It: What if Clyde could bring any number of items? Their weight would still have to total 35 pounds, but it wouldn't matter if he brought 6 items or 15. What combination of items might he bring?

4

Grades 3 & 4

NAME_____

Getting Around

Read each paragraph below. Match each trip described with the best form of transportation for that trip. Choose a form of transportation from the box and write it on the line.

| helicopter | jet | horse | train |
| small plane | boat | jeep | bicycle |

1. You will be traveling from one end of a long, winding river to the other. You really want to see this river up close. You should travel in a _____ .

2. You will be crossing an entire ocean as well as nearly half a continent. You want to do it quickly. You should travel by _____ .

3. You need to travel across 3 states. You need to travel quickly, but you also need to make a quick stop in 2 small towns. Your best bet would be a _____ .

4. You plan to travel through the southwestern United States. You will go directly across the desert. You will be on the road sometimes, and off it at others. You also want to see the desert up close, so you should go by _____ .

5. You have a lot of time, and being on the move is the whole point of your trip. You want to be able to stop whenever you want. You should travel by _____ .

6. You want to explore some jagged mountain peaks and a desert. You want to see the whole thing in one day, and maybe even land in a small field. Better take a _____ .

7. You have to cross the entire United States. But you don't mind taking your time because you want to see all the scenery along the way. You can take a _____ .

8. You want to explore a deep, long canyon close up. You will have to climb up and down some narrow, rocky trails to do this. You could use a _____ .

Since you can use each form of transportation only once, you may want to pencil in your answer choices. That way if you need to change some around, it will be easy.

Worldly Wise

Use prior knowledge

Grades 3 & 4

5

Worldly Wise
Read and use a map key

NAME _____

I Smell a Map!

The map on page 7 shows the imaginary state of Nosebend. Use the information in the key to fill in the blanks below. Then write the first letter of each answer to find out the kind of a map a frog might use.

> A map has a *key* that helps you read it. The key lists symbols that are found on the map and tells you what each one stands for.

1. Find a mountain. Write its name here. _____
2. Find a lake. Write its name here. _____
3. Find a park. Write its name here. _____
4. Find the capital. Write its name here. _____
5. Find a wetland. Write its name here. _____
6. Find a campground. Write its name here. _____
7. Find a racetrack. Write its name here. _____

What kind of map does a frog use? __ __ __ __ __ __ __

Can you match these symbols with the things they stand for?

Railroad

Airport

Port

Wildlife Refuge

Rest Area

Around the House: Ask your parents to help you locate a map of your local area. Find the key and look for key items on the map. Then try making a map of your neighborhood, your house, or your backyard and invent a key for it.

Grades 3 & 4

Worldly Wise

Read and use a map key

NAME

Make up your own symbols for these places. Add them to the map.

Baseball Stadium Playground School Waterfall
Public Beach Hospital

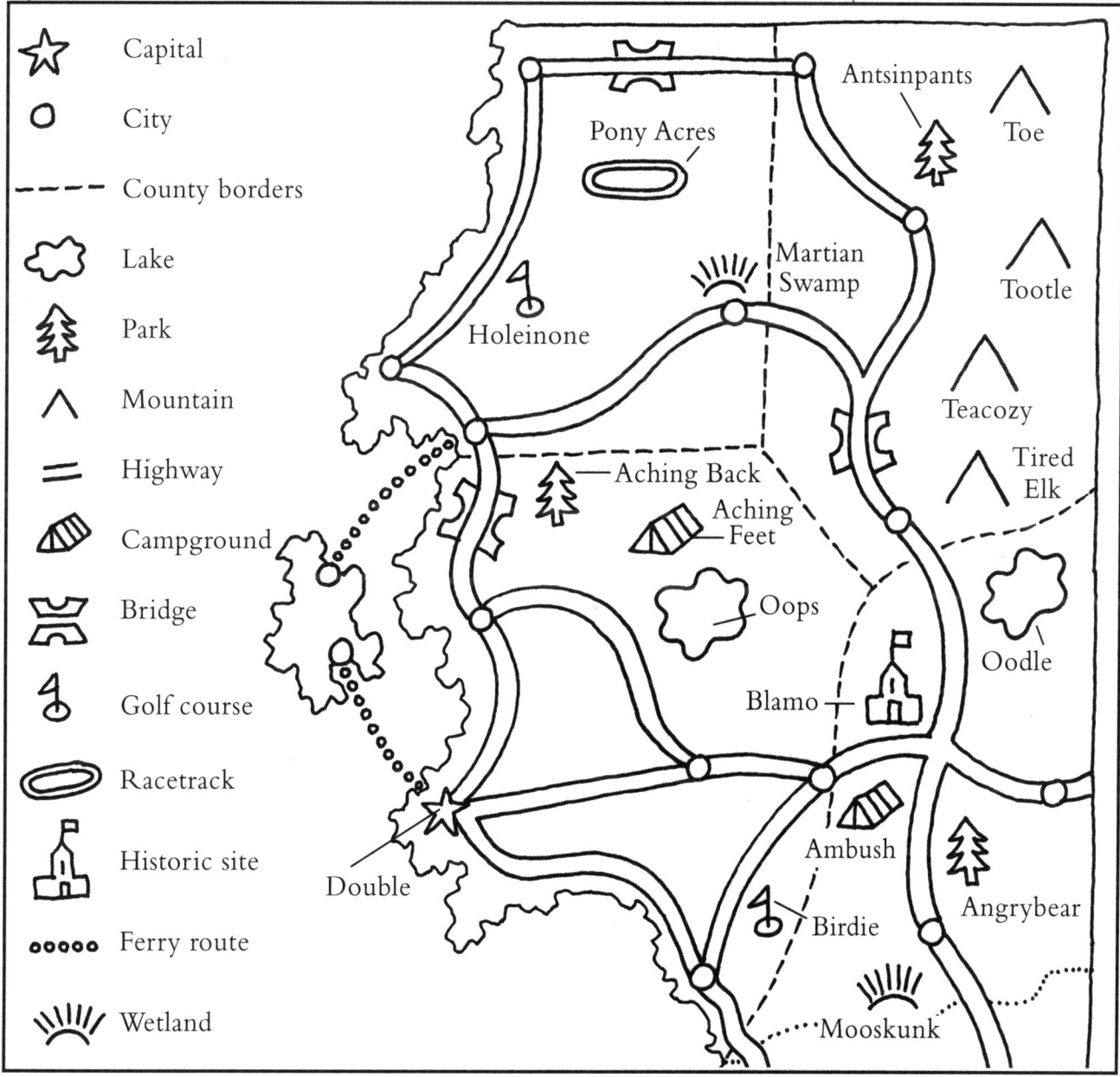

Grades 3 & 4

Worldly Wise

Use prior knowledge

NAME _____

Map Trap

Find a map of the United States in a road atlas or an encyclopedia. Then compare it with this map to help you spot all the mistakes.

You're about to set out on a drive across the United States. But your map has things mixed up on it—states have moved, and names have changed! See if you can circle 20 mistakes.

I knew you could "state" the right answers! OK, cut out the puzzle piece and add it to the frame on page 64.

Grades 3 & 4

In a State

Imelda Muzzle is traveling by plane to several states. Use these clues to follow her route. The clues tell what vowel sounds are in the names of the states she visited. Where will Imelda finally end up? Use a crayon to mark her path. Then draw a star at its end.

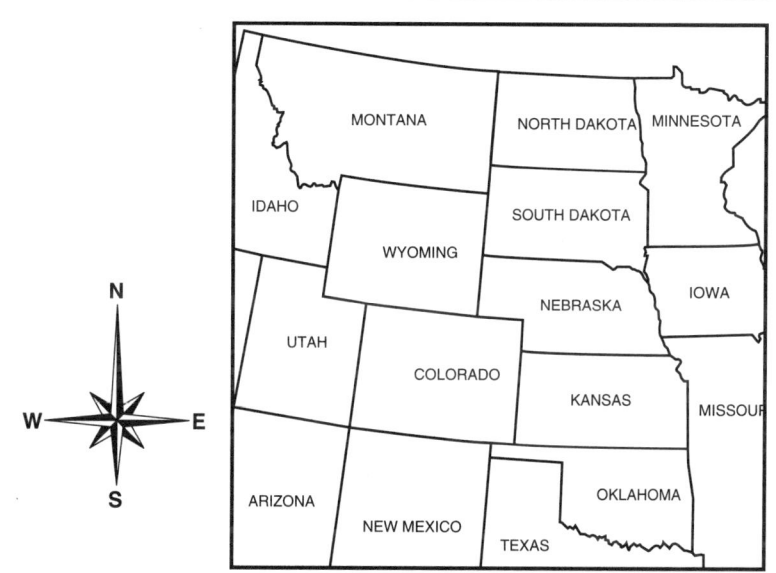

When a vowel is long, it sounds like it is saying its name. Use the chart below to help you remember how vowels sound when they are short.

Short Vowels
ă m<u>a</u>p
ĕ b<u>e</u>d
ĭ p<u>i</u>g
ŏ t<u>o</u>p
ŭ b<u>u</u>g

1. Imelda took off from a state whose name begins with a long *i* and ends with a long *o*. She flew south.
2. Her first stop was in a state whose name contains a long *o* in its third syllable.
3. After lunch, she took off again and flew to a state with a two-word name. The first word has the vowel sound heard in *boot*.
4. She flew north to a state whose name has a short *o* in its first syllable.
5. Next she continued north to a state whose name contains a short *a* in the middle syllable.
6. Her next-to-last stop was in a state with a two-word name. The first word includes the *ou* sound that is heard in *cow*.
7. Finally, Imelda landed for good. The name of the state she was in starts with a long *u*.

Worldly Wise
Follow directions

NAME _____

Way to Go!

Zak is planning to take his 15-foot-tall pet giraffe Minnie to see her relatives at the zoo. Which route should he use to get there? Read and obey the directions on the traffic signs as you find your way through this maze of streets. Draw a line to show the route.

Remember—there's a 15-foot-tall giraffe in that trailer. Don't go under any bridges that don't have enough clearance!

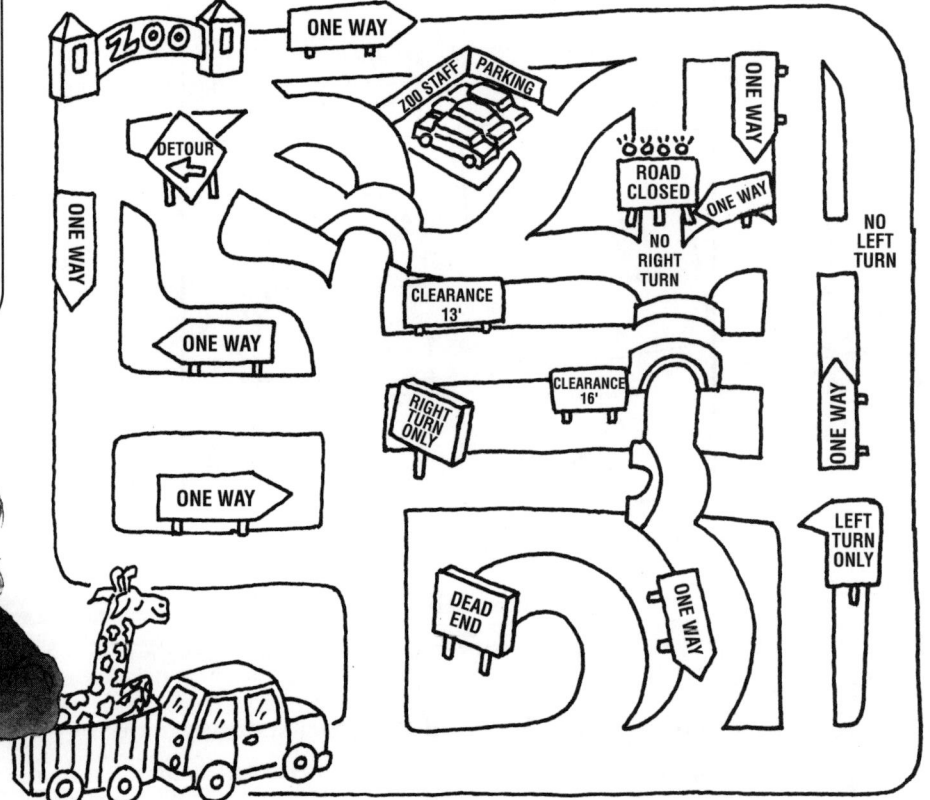

Around the House: What kinds of street signs can you find in your neighborhood? Some signs have words on them, such as "Stop." Others show only arrows or symbols. Bring a pad of paper with you when you travel in a car or on a bus, and copy the signs you see. Find out what they mean. Use the information to make a dictionary of road signs.

Grades 3 & 4

Birds of Paradise

Worldly Wise
Ecology and the environment

You're now visiting Hawaii, the tropical island state in the middle of the Pacific. Hawaii is home to many kinds of birds that are found nowhere else in the world—except in this word find! Look for the words that are in capital letters in the list below. Words go up, down, forward, and backward.

Bird Words
NENE—Hawaiian goose
ALALA—Hawaiian crow
PUEO—Hawaiian owl
OMAO—Hawaiian thrush
AMAKIHI—a little yellow-green bird
AKEPA—an orange-red songbird
PALILA—a yellow-and-gray songbird
APAPANE—a common red bird
IIWI—a bright-red bird with a curved bill
PUAIOHI—a brown-and-gray bird
OU—a plump bird with a yellow head

Fun Fact:
The Hawaiian alphabet uses only 12 letters: a, e, h, i, k, l, m, n, o, p, u, w. Can you find them all in the bird word list?

When you are done, write the leftover letters in the order you find them. They will spell a word that means "greetings" and "love" in Hawaiian.

Grades 3 & 4

Worldly Wise
Find synonyms

NAME _____

Herds of Words

Some synonyms mean the same thing, such as "little" and "small." Other synonyms are related but don't have exactly the same meaning, such as "big" and "gigantic."

Look at each vacation word below and see how many synonyms you can think of that are the same or are related in meaning. We did one for you to get you started.

trip	luggage	car
venture		
voyage		
vacation		
holiday		

hotel	restaurant	beach

Wow! I could list all the synonyms for "fantastic" here. Great job. OK, cut out this puzzle piece and add it to the frame on page 64.

boat	pictures	fun

Around the House: Play the game on this page with a friend or family member. Brainstorm a list of words together—or challenge your buddy, and see who can think of the most words! Think up other words to build on, too. You can also look up synonyms in a book called a thesaurus. Many computer programs even have a built-in thesaurus.

Word Pools

Worldly Wise
Make compound words

NAME _____

You're exploring two tidepools at the shore in Washington State. You find a huge starfish, but that's not all. You also find words that can be put together to form compound words. Match words from Pool 1 with words from Pool 2 to make 19 compound words. Write them on the lines. Hint: The words in the tidepools can be used more than once. That's right, so you'll need to try to match each word in Pool 1 with all the words in Pool 2 to be sure you don't miss any combinations.

Compound words are words that are made up of two or more words put together—like tidepool, seashore, *and* starfish!

Pool 1
jelly   butter   base
sea   dragon   basket
cat   eye
dog   foot

Pool 2
fish   bird   bean
horse   fly   weed
sled   cup   ball

What other compound words do you know? Write them here. _____

Grades 3 & 4

13

Worldly Wise
Read a table

From Tide to Tide

You've traveled south to a beach in Oregon. You plan to walk past Rocky Point and see Starfish Rock up close. Use the tide table to answer the questions on the next page and plan your adventures. If you don't read the table carefully, you may be trapped by the water!

Use a tide table before you plan a beach outing, because twice a day the tide comes in—which means the water crawls high up the shore. And twice a day the tide goes out—which means the water is low on the shore.

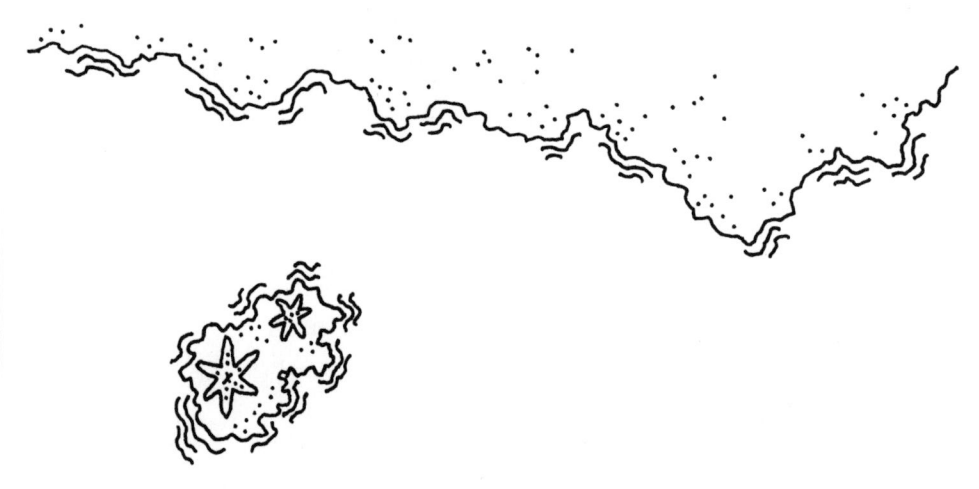

Day	Morning		Afternoon/Evening	
	High Tide	Low Tide	High Tide	Low Tide
Saturday	12:55 A.M.	7:31 A.M.	12:36 P.M.	6:31 P.M.
Sunday	1:38 A.M.	8:21 A.M.	2:01 P.M.	7:30 P.M.
Monday	2:13 A.M.	9:01 A.M.	3:13 P.M.	8:30 P.M.
Tuesday	2:45 A.M.	9:37 A.M.	4:06 P.M.	9:19 P.M.
Wednesday	3:12 A.M.	10:09 A.M.	4:55 P.M.	10:07 P.M.
Thursday	3:41 A.M.	10:39 A.M.	5:37 P.M.	10:49 P.M.
Friday	4:11 A.M.	11:13 A.M.	6:15 P.M.	11:31 P.M.

Grades 3 & 4

NAME _____

Worldly Wise
Read a table

1. What time will the low tide uncover Starfish Rock on Friday morning? _____
2. At what time will the second high tide of the day take place on Sunday? _____
3. At what time will the high tide block you from passing Rocky Point on Monday afternoon? _____
4. On what day and at what time will high tide be the earliest? _____
5. What time will the high tide block you from passing Rocky Point on Wednesday morning? _____
6. When will the high tide cover Starfish Rock on Friday morning? _____
7. When can you visit Starfish Rock on Saturday evening? _____
8. When will the tide be its highest on Thursday afternoon? _____
9. When will high tide cover Rocky Point on Wednesday afternoon? _____

It's time to cut out the puzzle piece. Glue or tape in place on page 64.

Write the first numeral of the times you picked in the boxes below. Match the numbers with the letters in the code box. Then unscramble the letters to find the answer to this riddle: "Why are shrimps and crabs so greedy?"

Because they're ☐ ☐ ☐ ☐ ☐ ☐ ☐ ☐ ☐ !
— — — — — — — — —

Code Box	
1 = L	4 = H
2 = I	5 = F
3 = S	6 = E

Grades 3 & 4   15

Worldly Wise
Multiply decimals

NAME _____

Fill It Up

Some travelers have stopped at Gus's Gas Station to fuel their cars. They have 5 kinds of gas to choose from. Find out how much each traveler paid for gas. Write the amount on the line.

To find out how much each traveler paid, multiply the number of gallons bought by the price of the gas. Don't forget to put the dollar sign and decimal point in your answer.

Sundance, my car, gets only the best. I bought 4 gallons of Ultra-ultra-ultrafuel today, so I paid _____

Gus's Regular: $1.25
Better: $1.35
Superduper: $1.47
Monsterpower: $1.62
Ultra-ultra-ultrafuel: $1.82

Monsterpower—that's the only kind of gas for my car. I bought 6 gallons. I paid _____ .

Superduper keeps my Cougar purring! I bought 7 gallons and paid _____ .

Keeping my old car running takes work, so I buy Better. I bought 8 gallons and paid _____ .

Gus's Regular gets me where I'm going. I bought 3 gallons and paid _____ .

16

Grades 3 & 4

There's Gold!

You are in California looking at an exhibit about three miners who have been panning for gold. See if you can figure out which of the miners has found the most gold. First, look at the fraction on each miner's shirt. Then look at the nuggets that miner has piled up. Find nuggets that contain fractions equivalent to the fraction on the miner's shirt. Color them in and you'll find the gold!.

The Wild West
Recognize equivalent fractions

The fractions $\frac{1}{5}$ and $\frac{3}{15}$ are equivalent because the numerator and denominator in the first fraction can each be multiplied by the same number (3) to give you the second fraction.

$$\frac{1\ (\times\ 3)}{5\ (\times\ 3)} = \frac{3}{15}$$

Grades 3 & 4

17

The Wild West

Multiply by 2-digit numbers

NAME _____

Read It and Sweat

If you choose to vacation in Death Valley, a desert area in southeastern California, be prepared for the heat. It gets really hot—even in the shade! Help Ima Roastin find the coolest spot to sit and enjoy a soda pop. Solve the multiplication problems. Then label the thermometers by the number that matches its temperature. Circle the thermometer with the coolest temperature.

You'll probably need to solve each problem on a piece of scratch paper. They will be easier if you set each one up vertically with the two-digit number on top.

1. 14 x 9 = _____
2. 8 x 15 = _____
3. 7 x 18 = _____
4. 6 x 22 = _____
5. 17 x 7 = _____
6. 59 x 2 = _____
7. 9 x 13 = _____
8. 44 x 3 = _____
9. 5 x 23 = _____

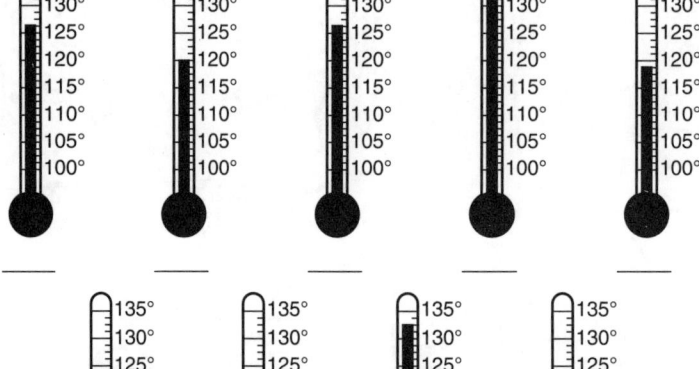

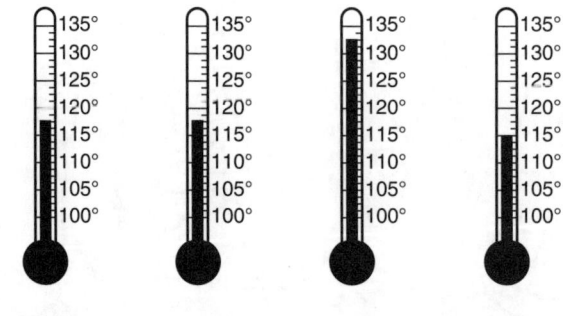

Around the House: What was the highest temperature ever recorded in your state? What was the lowest? Get your family and friends to guess. Then see if you can find the answers. Places to look include encyclopedias, books about your state, and the Internet.

18

Grades 3 & 4

How-Dee!

The Wild West
Define idioms

The sentences below have special words in them that are part of cowboy language. Test yourself and see how many of the bold-faced phrases below you can figure out. Circle the correct answer.

1. When a cowboy **cuts out** cattle, he
   a. snips cow shapes out of paper.
   b. works to remove one cow from a herd.
   c. brands cattle.

2. If a horse has **cow sense**, it
   a. can smell a cow from far away.
   b. is as smart as a cow.
   c. is good at helping round up and chase cows.

3. A **loco** cow is
   a. a crazy cow.
   b. the engine of a cattle train.
   c. a spotted cow.

4. When a cowgirl throws a **lariat**, she
   a. is playing a ball game.
   b. is trying to rope a cow.
   c. is angry.

5. A **chuck wagon** is
   a. a food wagon.
   b. a children's wagon.
   c. a wagon for sleeping in.

6. When a cowgirl rides a **bronc**, she is riding
   a. a bull.
   b. a motorcycle.
   c. a half-wild horse that bucks.

7. A **prairie chicken** is
   a. a kind of bird that lives on the grasslands.
   b. a cowboy who's scared of bulls.
   c. a very small calf.

8. If a cowboy says, "Where are my **chaps**?" he is looking for
   a. his friends.
   b. his leather pants that protect him from thorns.
   c. his ropes.

A word or phrase that doesn't mean exactly what it sounds like it means is called a *figure of speech*.

Some figures of speech are recognizable to only a certain group of people (like doctors, farmers, cowboys). Other figures of speech are common to everyone.

Grades 3 & 4

The Wild West

Note details, compare and contrast

NAME _____

Dig It!

Look at Didi's notes one characteristic at a time. Then look for a dinosaur description that includes that characteristic.

When you're finished, you should have one dinosaur that has all or most of its characteristics circled.

Dino-mite! Cut out this puzzle piece. Add it to the picture on page 64.

Dr. Didi Didanodon is digging in Dinosaur National Monument. She has found a new dinosaur fossil. Look at her notes. Then compare them with notes on dinosaur fossils that have already been discovered in Dinosaur National Monument. Use the clues to identify her dinosaur. Circle the dinosaur.

Didi's Dino Notes
1. lived during late Jurassic, about 142 million years ago
2. walked on 2 legs
3. had fangs—must be meat eater
4. hasn't found all bones but so far it's over 20 feet long
5. hands had 3 fingers
6. claws measured 1 foot

Dinosaur National Monument Official Notes

Dryosaurus: Plant eater, up to 13 feet long, walked on 2 legs, short arms with 5 clawed fingers	**Stegosaurus:** Plant eater, up to 30 feet long, spiky tail, flat plates on back, walked on 4 legs	**Apatosaurus:** Plant eater, up to 70 feet long, long, thick neck, long tail, walked on 4 legs
Allosaurus: Meat eater, up to 36 feet long, short arms with 3 fingers and 6-inch claws, walked on 2 legs	**Ceratosaurus:** Meat eater, up to 20 feet long, short arms with 4 fingers and big claws, walked on 2 legs	**Torvosaurus:** Meat eater, up to 33 feet long, short arms with 3 fingers and 12-inch claws, walked on 2 legs

Grades 3 & 4

NAME_____

Park That Conjunction

The Wild West

Combine sentences with comma and conjunction

Jamie Puptent is on a camping trip in Yellowstone National Park. He's writing an essay about his trip, but he's having some trouble joining his sentences. Help him out by picking conjunctions from the list and putting them into the sentences.

More than one conjunction may make sense, but each conjunction is used only once.

That means you may want to change an answer after you have already begun, so be sure to use pencil.

| so | but | or | and | yet |

1. Wolves were set free in Yellowstone, _____ they are now raising pups.
2. You can visit in summer and hike, _____ you can visit in winter and go cross-country skiing.
3. A million or more people visit Yellowstone every year, _____ I feel as if I'm exploring a place that's wild and free.
4. The bison in the park look tame, _____ they're really wild animals.
5. The geyser Old Faithful erupts almost every 80 minutes, _____ people know just when to arrive and wait for it.

Now think about a place you've visited, and write some sentences of your own using conjunctions. _____
_____
_____
_____

Around the House: Play a conjunction game with your family or friends. Divide the group into pairs. Have each player write a complete sentence without showing it to his or her partner. Each pair then takes a turn sharing their sentences and choosing a conjunction that can link their sentences sensibly. Set a timer and give each pair no more than 15 seconds to choose an answer!

Grades 3 & 4

The Wild West
Write a personal narrative

NAME _____

My Vacation

Think about a vacation you have taken. What did you see and do? What made it fun? What made it unusual? What made it exciting? Answer the questions below. Then on another piece of paper, write a personal narrative about a trip you've taken.

A *personal narrative* is a piece of writing about an event in your life. Because it is personal, you can include your thoughts and opinions as you tell about what happened or what you did.

Where did you go? _____
Who were you traveling with? _____
When was this trip? _____
How old were you? _____
How did you feel about going on this trip? _____
Did your feelings change as the trip went on? _____
What was the funniest thing that happened on your trip? _____
_____
What did you see there? _____
What was the weather like on this trip? _____
If you could take this trip again, would you change it? _____
If so, how? _____
_____
_____
_____

Around the House: Have you ever kept a journal? A journal is a record of your day-to-day life—the things you've done. It is also a place to record your thoughts and feelings. A journal can be a lifelong personal narrative. Start one if you haven't already. Any notebook can serve as a journal. Or try keeping a travel log instead. That's a journal that is just about your travels.

Grades 3 & 4

NAME_____

On the Road

The Wild West
Determine mileage

While on vacation, Heather Fanbelt rented a car to see the sights. Read about her trip. Use the information to figure out where her hotel was. Circle the city on the map.

On the first day of her trip, she drove to Whiffle and then back to her motel.
On the second day, she drove to Caboose, then to Hophog, and then back to her motel.
On the third day, she drove to Picklesville and back.
She drove a total of 62 miles.

> Look at the map. The little numbers written next to the roads tell you how many miles lie between the two cities.

> As you're adding distances, you must remember one thing: Heather always chooses the shortest distance between two places.

Map shows:
- Snorting Elk
- Hophog
- Whiffle
- Caboose
- Node
- Picklesville
- Lower Upsville

Distances: Snorting Elk to Whiffle: 14; Whiffle to Hophog: 6; Hophog to Caboose: 5; Snorting Elk to Node: 12; Whiffle to Lower Upsville: 11; Caboose to Lower Upsville: 10; Node to Lower Upsville: 10; Picklesville to Lower Upsville: 5.

Around the House: Ask your parents if they have a road atlas. If not, find one at the library. Look at the maps. See if you can figure out the distance between your home and places in the United States that you would like to visit.

Grades 3 & 4   **23**

The Wild West

Compare decimals up to hundredths

NAME _____

Hee-Haw!

Lonesome Joe took a trek through the Grand Canyon on his vacation, but now he's more lonesome than ever. You see, he's stuck at the bottom of the canyon. Draw a path to help him and his mule find their way to the top. When you get to a fork in the trail, look at the decimals. Take the path with the greater decimal.

> When you compare decimals, look at the tenths place first. Then look at the hundredths place.

> .6 is greater than .16 because 6 tenths is greater than one tenth.

> Cut out this piece and glue or tape it in place on page 64.

Check Yourself: Look at the decimal numbers you chose. They get larger as you travel along the correct path. If any get smaller, you've gone the wrong way. Try again!

NAME _____

Speechless in Dakota!

The Wild West

Use consonant blends and digraphs

If you were to visit South Dakota, you might want to visit a famous monument called Mt. Rushmore. Four presidents' faces are carved into the side of this mountain. Here, each president is trying to tell you something about himself. But somebody has stolen letters from their speeches. They're missing consonant blends and digraphs from the beginnings and ends of their words. See if you can find them in the list below. Then put them into the speeches where they belong. Cross out each blend or digraph in the list as you use it.

Beginning Blends and Digraphs:			Ending Blends and Digraphs:	
ch	pr	st	ck	rd
fr	sh	th	nd	rl
gr	sh	tr	nt	rst
pl	sl	tw	rd	th
pr	sp	ch		
sp				

I'm George Washington, the first ___esident of the United States. I served from 1789 to 1797. By the way, that ___ory about how I cut down a ___erry tree isn't really ___ue!

I'm Theodore Roosevelt, president number ___enty-six. I am famous for saying "___eak softly and carry a big sti___." I was the fir___ president to ride in a ___ane.

I'm Thomas Jefferson. I was ___esident number ___ree. When I bought a large ___unk of la___, it became known as the Louisiana Purchase. I had a pet mockingbi___ that would sit on my ___oulder!

I'm Abraham Lincoln, the sixteen___ preside___. I led the nation during the Civil War. A little gi___ gave me the suggestion to ___ow a bea___! I gave a ___eech that set all ___aves ___ee. Sad to say, I was ___ot and killed.

Grades 3 & 4

25

The Wild West

Divide by 1-digit numbers

NAME _____

Full Plates

While traveling around the country, Reed A. Tag loves to look at cars and their license plates. One day he wondered what would happen to the United States if everybody bought a pink car. He wrote an answer for his riddle but buried it in the license plates below. Here's how you can find the answer:

1. Divide the number in each license plate by the number in parenthesis.
2. Write the answer on the line.
3. Use your answers, from least to greatest, to put the groups of letters in the right order in the boxes at the bottom of the page.

Use long division to find the answer to each problem. Then check your division with multiplication. For example, if 441 ÷ 3 = 147, then 147 x 3 must be equal to 441.

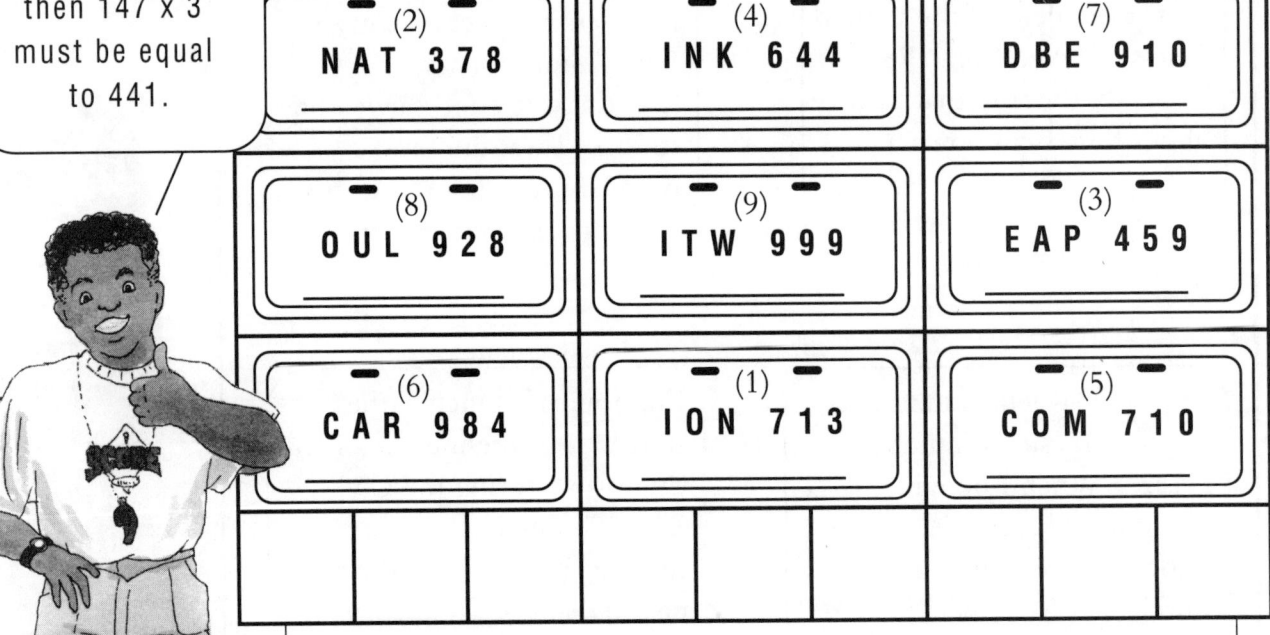

(2) NAT 378	(4) INK 644	(7) DBE 910
(8) OUL 928	(9) ITW 999	(3) EAP 459
(6) CAR 984	(1) ION 713	(5) COM 710

Around the House: See if you can find cars with license plates from different states. Make it a game and challenge a friend or family member. See who can find cars from the most states.

The Name Game

The Wild West
Identify antonyms

Auntie Nim likes to travel. She visits lots of towns and keeps track of their names. She likes to visit towns with names that are antonyms of the ones she's already seen. For example, if she visits Boring, Oregon, she then likes to visit a place with a name like Brilliant, Alabama!

See if you can help Auntie Nim with her odd travel plans. List 1 shows the U.S. towns she has visited. List 2 has towns that could be their antonyms. Look for words in their names that are antonyms of words in List 1. Use a dictionary to help you, if you wish. Draw a line between the antonyms.

Antonyms are words that have opposite meanings.

List 1	List 2
Kicking Horse, MT	Boiling Springs, PA
Sour Lake, TX	Coldwater, MO
Hot Coffee, MS	Deadhorse, AK
Normal, IL	Easthampton, MA
Evening Star, AR	Little Rock, AR
Nice, CA	Lowpoint, IL
Summersville, MT	Morning Sun, AR
Black Horse, OH	Peace Valley, MO
Sunrise, FL	Peculiar, MO
Advance, NC	Pleasureville, PA
Big Rock, VA	Retreat, GA
Painesville, OH	Savage, MT
Cold Springs, KY	Sunset, AR
Westhampton, NY	Sweetwater, TN
Warfield, KY	White Horse, NM
High Point, MO	Winterville, NC

Grades 3 & 4

The Wild West
Read a map using a grid

NAME _____

Hot Off the Grid

A grid is a set of crisscrossing lines that covers a map. Each line is identified by a letter or number. When looking for a town, you must look in the index to find what lines the town is near. Now use the grid to find the answers to these riddles. (Each answer is the name of a real town in Nebraska!) We've given you codes that tell you where to find the answers on the map on the next page.

Look to see where the line marked 3 and the line marked C meet. There you will find the town of Chambers.

1. What towns are filled with wood-chewing animals? (1-I and 7-G) _____
2. What town might chefs like to visit? (10-H) _____
3. What town sounds very dangerous? (3-F) _____
4. In what town is it hard to sleep? (8-B) _____
5. In what town might you go for a swim? (3-F) _____
6. What towns might flower lovers like? (4-H and 5-E) _____

7. In what town might the sky look a bit different? (4-I) _____

8. In what town would your arrow be of no use? (1-E) _____

9. What town thinks it is the best? (5-I) _____
10. What town is very welcoming? (7-G) _____
11. What town might librarians like? (4-B) _____
12. What town do some dog lovers like? (2-B) _____
13. In what town is nothing hidden? (6-B) _____

28

Grades 3 & 4

NAME_____

The Wild West
Read a map using a grid

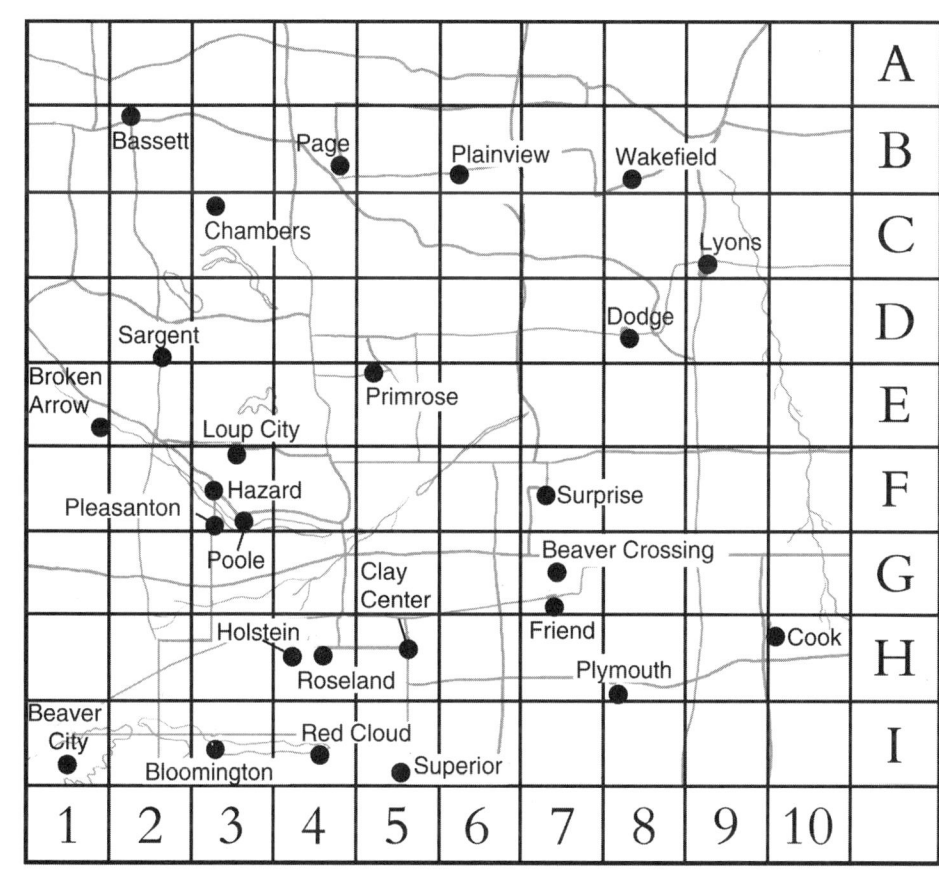

A-1! That's your grid number! Now it's time to cut out that puzzle piece and find its home on page 64. Don't forget to glue or tape it in place.

Grades 3 & 4

29

The Wild West
Write a story

NAME _____

What's In a Name?

Your town might have been named after an unusual person or a mysterious event from the past. Or maybe your town was named after a special part of the land that surrounds it.

Just look for an interesting name, and let your imagination run!

On pages 27 to 29, you saw lots of towns with interesting names. How do you think these towns got their names? Pick one and make up a story about how it was named. Write your story here. You can also write on your own paper if you want to create a longer story with pictures.

_____
_____
_____
_____
_____
_____
_____
_____
_____
_____
_____
_____
_____
_____
_____
_____
_____

Around the House: What is your town's name? How did it get its name? You can find out by researching it at your local library. Write a nonfiction story (a true story) about how your town got its name. If you like, you can also invent a story that is fiction (make-believe) about how your town got its name.

Make a Map

Find a map of the United States in an encyclopedia or an atlas. Use it to draw your own U.S. map below. Then look at the features listed in the box. See if you can find an example of each feature on the map in the reference book. Then add it to your own map on this page.

Did you know that the United States stretches about 2,807 miles from the west coast to the east coast and measures about 1,598 miles from north to south?

And that doesn't even include Hawaii and Alaska, which aren't attached to the other 48 states!

Where can you see:

a volcano?	a delta?	a canyon?
a mountain range?	a desert?	an ocean?
a river?	a prairie?	a lake?

These Great States

Identify geological structures

Grades 3 & 4

These Great States

Perform computations with

NAME _____

Measure Up!

Zak is taking his 15-foot giraffe Minnie to see some very tall things in the United States and Canada. Some of them are described below. Use the clues in the boxes to answer the questions on the next page. It will really help Zak and Minnie to enjoy their trip.

Name: Big Tex **What it is:** a giant cowboy statue that stands tall at the Texas State Fair **Height:** 52 feet	**Name:** Empire State Building **What it is:** a skyscraper in New York City **Height:** 1,472 feet	**Name:** Sears Tower **What it is:** a skyscraper in Chicago, IL **Height:** 1,707 feet
Name: CN Tower **What it is:** an observation and communication tower in Toronto, Ontario **Height:** 1,815 feet	**Name:** Gateway to the West **What it is:** a giant arch in St. Louis, MO, the world's tallest monument **Height:** 630 feet	**Name:** "Battle of San Jacinto" monument **What it is:** a column near Houston, TX, that honors the end of the Texas Revolution **Height:** 570 feet tall
Name: Washington Monument **What it is:** a monument in Washington, DC **Height:** about 555 feet	**Name:** Statue of Liberty **What it is:** statue on a pedestal in New York's harbor **Height:** about 306 feet	**Name:** General Sherman Tree **What it is:** a giant sequoia in Sequoia National Park, CA **Height:** about 275 feet
Name: "Tall Tree" Coast Redwood **What it is:** a redwood tree in northern California **Height:** about 365 feet	**Name:** Space Needle **What it is:** a tower with a restaurant on top in Seattle, WA **Height:** 605 feet	**Name:** "World's Largest Coffee Pot" **What it is:** a water tower in Stanton, IA **Height:** 125 feet

NAME_____

These Great States

Perform computations with measurements

1. About how many Minnies would it take to reach the height of the "World's Largest Coffee Pot"? _____
2. Which is the shortest of the 12 things listed on page 32? _____ Which is the tallest? _____
3. What is the difference in the heights of the two attractions mentioned in question number 2? _____
4. About how many models of Big Tex would it take to reach the height of the Gateway to the West? _____
5. How many feet shorter is the Washington Monument than the "Battle of San Jacinto" monument? _____
6. Which is taller—the tallest redwood or the tallest sequoia? _____ _____ By how many feet? _____
7. How many feet taller is the Sears Tower than the Empire State Building? _____
8. How many feet shorter is the Sears Tower than the CN Tower? _____
9. How many Space Needles does it take to equal the height of the CN Tower? _____
10. About how many Minnies would it take to reach the height of the General Sherman Tree? _____
11. How much taller is the Statue of Liberty than Big Tex? _____
12. How tall are you? _____ How many of you would it take to approximately equal the height of the Empire State Building? _____ The Washington Monument? _____ The "World's Largest Coffee Pot"? _____

Remember, Minnie is 15 feet tall. So to figure out how many Minnies it would take to reach the height of Big Tex, you would have to divide 52 by 15.

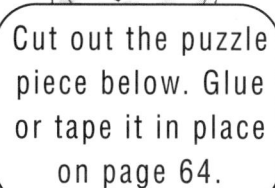

Cut out the puzzle piece below. Glue or tape it in place on page 64.

Around the House: Measure the heights of all your family members. Keep track of all the heights on a paper chart taped to a wall or door frame. Every now and then, measure everybody again to see if they have grown.

Grades 3 & 4

These Great States

Draw a line graph and plot points

NAME _____

Stack 'em Up

To make a line graph you must first mark the height of each attraction by putting a dot on the graph above its name. Use the numbers going up the side of the graph to help you plot these points.

When you are done, draw lines between the dots.

Use the information on page 32 to make a line graph about the tall things people can visit in the United States. First, write the height of each attraction next to its name in this box. That way you won't have to keep flipping to page 32 as you are making your graph.

Big Tex _____
"World's Largest Coffee Pot" _____
General Sherman tree _____
The Statue of Liberty _____
"Tall Tree" Coast Redwood _____
Washington Monument _____
"Battle of San Jacinto" monument _____
Space Needle _____
Gateway to the West _____
Empire State Building _____
Sears Tower _____
CN Tower _____

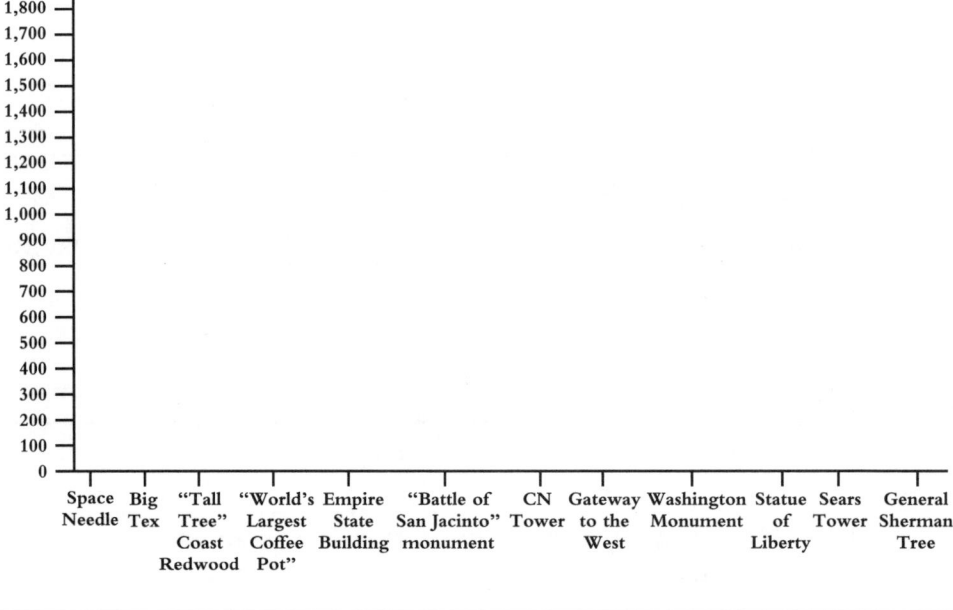

34

Grades 3 & 4

NAME_____

These Great States

Estimate height in feet

How Tall Is Tall?

People are always on the lookout for the tallest trees. New record breakers are often discovered. Here is one way you can measure a tall tree without climbing it!

1. Find a stick that is about as long as your arm.
2. Stretch your arm straight out. Hold the bottom of the stick so it points straight up.
3. Have a friend guide you as you step backward away from the tree. Keep walking until the top of your stick lines up with the top of the tree. Then make sure the bottom of your stick lines up with the bottom of the tree.
4. Mark the spot you are standing on. Then take "giant steps" back to the tree, counting as you go. This is called "pacing out" the distance.
5. About how many feet long is your "giant step," or stride?_____ Multiply the length of your stride by how many "giant steps" you took. The answer you get is about the height of the tree. _____

Around the House: If you find a cut, fallen tree, see if you can count the rings in the cross-section of the trunk. If there are too many to count, just count how many are in one inch. Then measure the trunk from its center to its outside. Multiply the number of inches by how many rings you count in one inch, and you will have the approximate age of the tree!

Pacing out a tree's height might not work very well in a crowded forest. But you can still discover some interesting measurements.

Grades 3 & 4

These Great States

Divide words into syllables

NAME _____

Just Add Milk

> Use slash marks to divide each word into syllables. That will help you keep track of the clues as you go.

Nick Atnoon is a big cereal fan, and he's visiting Battle Creek, Michigan, the world's leading producer of breakfast cereal. He wants to stock up on his favorite cereal. But he's so dazzled by the choices, he's totally forgotten which cereal is his favorite! Help him out by using the clues below to figure out which cereal he should buy. Dividing the words in the cereal names into syllables is the key to figuring it out.

> I can tell you're a real bran— I mean brain! Now cut out this puzzle piece, and add it to page 64.

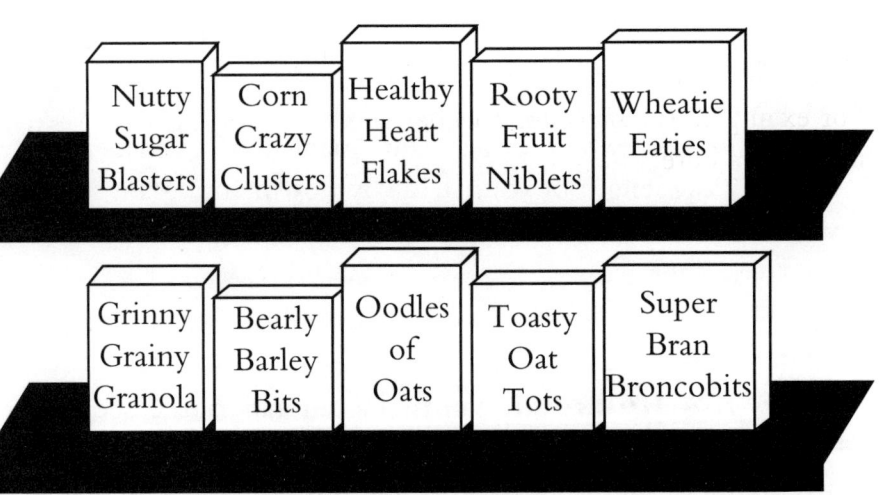

Nutty Sugar Blasters | Corn Crazy Clusters | Healthy Heart Flakes | Rooty Fruit Niblets | Wheatie Eaties

Grinny Grainy Granola | Bearly Barley Bits | Oodles of Oats | Toasty Oat Tots | Super Bran Broncobits

The Clues:
The cereal has 3 words in its name.
The cereal has 1 syllable in the second word of its name.
The cereal has 2 syllables in the first word of its name.
The cereal has more than 2 syllables in the last word of its name.

Nick's Favorite: _____

Around the House: Look at the cereals in your kitchen cupboard. How many were made in Battle Creek, MI?

Grades 3 & 4

These Great States

Use figurative language

NAME _____

Word Pictures

You can use figurative language to write about different kinds of weather. Follow the directions below to describe the snow, wind, sun, and rain.

1. Use a simile. A simile compares two things by using the words *like* or *as*. For example, *The snow covered the yard like a blanket.* Make up your own similes here:

   The snow lay on our house like a _____.

   The sun felt as hot as a _____ on my back.

   Invent some more similes and write them here: _____
   _____

2. Use a metaphor. A metaphor compares two things without using *like* or *as*. For example, *The snow was a white blanket covering the yard.* Make up your own metaphors here:

   The snow was a _____ that buried our house.

   The sun was a _____ heating up my back.

   Invent some more metaphors and write them here: _____
   _____

3. Use onomatopoeia! That's using words that sound like their meanings. For example, *The snow swished and swirled around me as the wind whistled.* Try using an onomatopoeia in these sentences:

   The snow _____ against the window.

   The rain _____ on the roof.

   Write some more words that are examples of onomatopoeia here: _____
   _____

Grades 3 & 4

These Great States

Inventory plants in local environments

NAME _____

On the Trail

A plant magazine has asked you to travel across the United States photographing plants in their natural environments. Can you be the first to complete the trip successfully? Find a friend, play this game, and find out!

First, you'll have to get two pennies and a button or another small object for each player.

Then look carefully at the chart to see how to play this game.

Game board spaces:

- You found the 4,600-year-old bristlecone pines. Move forward 3 spaces!
- You stop someone from picking a trillium. Roll again!
- Fly to "Hawaii" to photograph rare silver-sword plant!
- You squash rare alpine plants on Mt. Rainier in Washington. Lose 1 turn.
- You find Joshua trees in Mojave Desert. Move forward 2!
- You hurt your neck gazing up at tall redwoods in California. Go back 1.
- Step on rare woodland orchid—lose 1 turn.
- Admire a blue columbine flower in Colorado's mountains. Move forward 2.
- Admire saguaro cacti in Sonoran Desert. Move forward 1.
- You find a pipsissewa flower in a midwestern forest! Roll again!
- A bison chases you in Yellowstone National Park! Go back 2.
- Ow! A bee stings you. Lose 1 turn.
- See 6-foot tall "Queen of the Prairie" plant. Move forward 2.

START

38

Grades 3 & 4

NAME_____

These Great States

Inventory plants in local environments

What You Do:
1. Toss the pennies to see how far you can move.
   If they both land heads up, move one space.
   If they both land tails up, move two spaces.
   If one is heads and the other tails, move three spaces.
2. Move your playing piece around the board. Follow any rules that appear in the spaces you land on.
3. The first to reach the garden wins.

Around the House: What kind of plants can you find in your backyard or local park? Borrow a field guide from the library and find out! Do any of the plants grow in only your part of the world?

Grades 3 & 4

These Great States

Round to the nearest 100

NAME _____

Round 'em Up

You're visiting Wisconsin, America's Dairyland! Tons of milk is produced here. It is also the number-one cheese producer in the United States. Take this trivia quiz and see how much you know about cows. Here's how to find the right answers:

1. Add the numbers in the problem below each question.
2. Round the sum to the nearest hundred.
3. The rounded number tells you which answer is right.
4. Circle the answer to the question.

Cowabunga! Great work! Before you move on, take a second to cut out this puzzle piece. Add it to the frame on page 64. Glue or tape it in place.

A. A cow spends about how many hours a day chewing?
   96 + 87 = _____
   100   8 hours   200   14 hours   180   3 hours

B. How many squirts of milk does it take to fill a pail?
   112 + 49 = _____
   100   600 squirts   600   150 squirts   200   350 squirts

C. About how much cheese does the average American eat in a year?
   77 + 185 = _____
   300   26 pounds   200   15 pounds   600   48 pounds

D. How many pounds of grass does a cow eat in a day?
   357 + 329 = _____
   700   100 pounds   800   200 pounds   900   20 pounds

E. About how many cattle live in the United States?
   481 + 206 = _____
   700   100,000,000   800   10,000,000   900   1,000,000,000

F. About how much does an adult Holstein cow weigh?
   220 + 529 = _____
   700   1,500 pounds   800   3,000 pounds   400   500 pounds

G. How many gallons of milk does a cow make in a day?
   100 + 264 + 183 = _____
   400   1 gallon   500   10 gallons   600   100 gallons

40

Grades 3 & 4

NAME_____

Wish You Were Here

These Great States

Write a friendly letter

Have you ever written a postcard and sent it to a friend? Make a sample of a postcard here. Draw a picture of a place you have visited (or would like to visit) on the front of the card. Then write a message to a friend on the back of the card.

Front of Card

Back of Card

Dear _____,

Postcards often have pictures of places on them. People buy them while traveling to write about their trip.

Grades 3 & 4

These Great States
Word play and puns

NAME _____

Pun State

All of these riddles use puns, but before you can tell them, you'll have to fill in the blanks. Look at the riddles. Then decide which state's name belongs in each riddle.

1. What did ___Tennessee___ ?
   The same thing that ___Arkansas___ !
2. What did Bob say when he figured out his _____?
   "Gee, _____ lot of money!"
3. Do you know how to get to the North Pole? Neither do I, but _____ reindeer if I see one!
4. What did _____ to the party?
   She wore her _____ !
5. What do you buy if you're just a little thirsty? A _____
6. Is Ore still here? No, _____
7. A gardener had a helper named Ida. But Ida simply would not use a rake. What should the gardener do? Let _____ and do the raking himself!
8. What did the teacher call Mr. Sippi's wife? _____
9. What state is best for cars? _____
10. Where should you take your laundry? _____

A *pun* is a funny twist on a word or words.
It makes a joke by playing with the sounds of words.

State Box

Washington	Idaho	Delaware
Texas	New Jersey	~~Arkansas~~
Mississippi	Minnesota	Oregon
Rhode Island	Iowa	
~~Tennessee~~	Alaska	

42

Grades 3 & 4

Gone to Pizzas

Evie Backpack is vacationing with her friends at a campsite. They couldn't start a fire, so they decided to order pizzas for dinner. They ordered 4 pizzas: one pepperoni, one anchovy, one pepper and one sprout-and-mushroom. While the kids were pitching their tents, some animals snuck out of the woods and stole their food! See if you can figure out answers to the questions at the bottom of the page. Use the clues to help you.

pepperoni

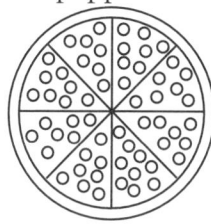

Clues

- A bear stole $\frac{1}{2}$ the pepperoni pizza, $\frac{1}{4}$ of the anchovy pizza, and $\frac{3}{8}$ of the pepper pizza.
- A crow stole $\frac{1}{8}$ of the pepper pizza and $\frac{1}{4}$ of the anchovy pizza.
- A raccoon stole $\frac{1}{8}$ of the pepperoni pizza, $\frac{3}{8}$ of the anchovy pizza, $\frac{3}{8}$ of the pepper pizza, and $\frac{1}{8}$ of the sprout-and-mushroom pizza.
- A moose ate $\frac{5}{8}$ of the sprout-and-mushroom pizza.

anchovy

pepper

sprout-and-mushroom

Shade in the pizzas to help you figure out just how much of each pizza the animals ate.

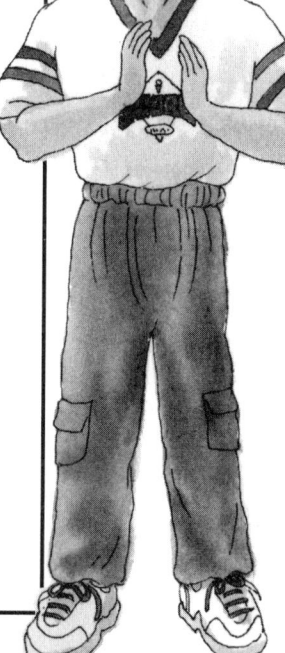

1. Which animal had the most pizza? _____
   How many slices did it eat? _____
2. Which animal had the least pizza? _____
   How many slices did it eat? _____
3. How many slices were left for the humans? _____
   What kind were they? _____

These Great States

Use fractions in word problems

Grades 3 & 4

43

These Great States
Add thousands

NAME _____

Simply Ducky

You're at the Iowa State Fair. You decide to play "Better Duck, Duck!" In this game, you throw a ball at a moving target of a metal duck. Here's what you do:

1. Add the numbers in one of the balls.
2. Look at the duck that is directly across the board from the ball. Do the numbers in the ball add up to the number that is on the duck? If they do, your aim is great! Draw a straight line between the ball and the duck.
3. Do this for all the balls. If the ball's numbers do not add up to the duck's number, don't draw a line.
4. Circle all the ducks you hit. Add up their numbers. The answer will tell you which prize you have won.
5. The letters that you did not cross out answer this riddle: "How many ducks can you put into an empty tub?"

Before you move ahead, cut out this puzzle piece. Then glue or tape it in the frame on page 64.

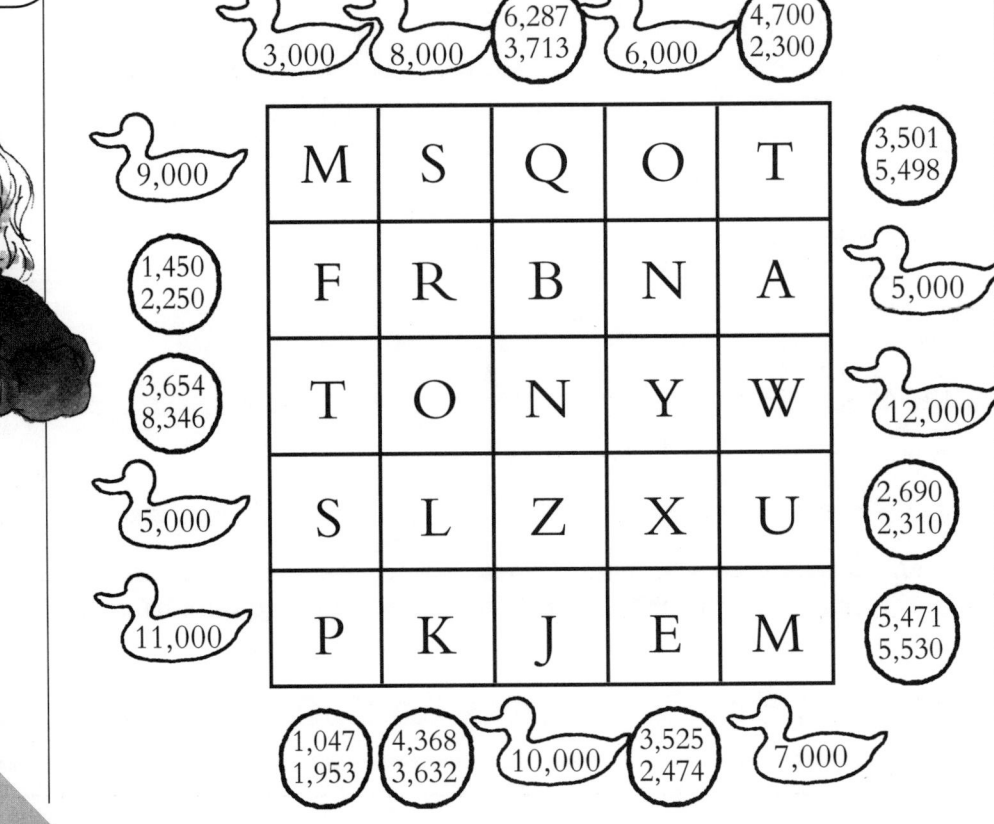

44

Grades 3 & 4

NAME _____

State of Mine

These Great States
Find information in an encyclopedia

People who visit your state would probably enjoy learning about it. Do you know what your state bird is? How about your state flower? Flag? Song? Find out this information about your state and fill in the blanks below. Then draw pictures to illustrate your answers.

My state's name is _____ .

The state bird is _____ .

Here is a picture of it:

The state flower is _____ .

Here is a picture of it:

The state flag looks like this:

The state song is _____ .

An *encyclopedia* is a great place for finding information like this. Find the volume that contains the letter your state begins with. Then find the pages about your state.

Why do you think your state chose the bird it did? Write your thoughts here. _____

What do the symbols on your state flag mean? _____

Grades 3 & 4

Here, There, Everywhere

Identify planets in the solar system

NAME _____

Blast-off!

Lucy Skyskipper is in space. While she's there, she's taking a good look around. Help her identify the planets she sees. Look at the planet clues below. Write the planet name next to the planet you think it goes with.

Out of this world! Now cut out the puzzle piece and put it in place on page 64.

Saturn is famous for its many rings.
Pluto is the farthest from the sun.
Venus is between Mercury and Earth.
Mars is next to the largest planet.
Earth is the third planet from the sun.
Mercury is the smallest planet.
Neptune has rings but is smaller than Saturn.
Uranus is tilted on its side, and so are its rings.
Jupiter is the largest planet.

Grades 3 & 4

Sounds Like ...

K.C. is writing a letter to her friend about her trip to Tennessee, but she has left out some words. Fill in each blank using a word in the list below. Each pair of words is made up of homophones—words that sound alike but are spelled differently and have different meanings.

ate/eight   piece/peace   bear/bare   hole/whole
tail/tale   hear/here   deer/dear

_____ Amy,

   We are in Paris, Tennessee, for "The World's Largest Fish Fry." About 8,500 pounds of catfish were cooked for this event! I _____ almost all of my fish except its _____ . My family was hungry, so all together we gobbled up _____ fish. Afterwards, I was so full I couldn't even eat a tiny _____ of cake. We left the feast to walk in the woods.

   I saw a _____ with huge antlers, but thank goodness I didn't see a _____ . Timmy fell in a _____ and had to be pulled out! Then we went to a lake. I ran on the sand in my _____ feet. Later, an old man asked us if we would like to _____ a _____ about Casey Jones, a famous railroad engineer and hero from Tennessee. It was a great story.

   This was a fun trip. Mom says she likes the _____ and quiet of our cabin. I slept outdoors the _____ time! I hope we come _____ again some day.

Your friend,
K.C.

How can you tell which word is the right one to use? Just look up one of the two words in a dictionary!

Here, There, Everywhere

Use homophones

Grades 3 & 4

Here, There, Everywhere

Distinguish fact from opinion

NAME _____

Says You!

A fact is something that can be proven.

An opinion is an idea or point of view. It tells how someone thinks or feels about something.

Hey, that was a snap! Now it's time to cut out this puzzle piece.

Allie Gator visited an alligator park in Florida. She heard many facts—but she also heard some opinions. Help Allie decide which statements are facts and which are opinions. Put an F on the line below each fact and an O on the line below each opinion.

- An alligator keeps growing throughout its life. _____
- It's better to be a warm-blooded animal than a cold-blooded one. _____
- An alligator's lower teeth are hidden inside its mouth when it shuts its jaws. _____
- An alligator grows new teeth to replace old ones all its life. _____
- Alligators are quite beautiful. _____
- An alligator uses its tail to swim. _____
- Alligators build nests out of leaves, branches, and mud piled into a heap. _____
- The alligator is the most interesting animal in America. _____
- Alligators don't have any feelings. _____
- An alligator can grow to be 20 feet long. _____
- A mother alligator may help her babies break out of their shells and even hold the little ones in her mouth for safety. _____
- Alligators are frightening animals. _____

48

Grades 3 & 4

NAME _____

Here, There, Everywhere
Write a short research report

Creature Feature

Think of a place in the United States you would like to visit. What interesting animal might you see there? Find out some facts about the animal, and write a short report to tell about it. Use the questions below to get started.

Look up the animal in an encyclopedia. But to find really amazing facts, you'll need other books. Look for books about American animals and books just about your animal. Use field guides and magazine articles, too!

What is the name of your animal? _____

What state or states does it live in? _____

Where would you be likely to see this animal? for example, a swamp? the woods? the ocean? _____

How big or little is it? _____

What does your animal eat? _____

What other animals live near your animal? _____

What are 3 facts about your animal that you think are amazing? _____
_____
_____

Begin your research report here. Add extra pieces of paper to write more. At the end, list the books and other sources, or materials, from which you got your facts. _____
_____
_____
_____
_____
_____

Grades 3 & 4

Here, There, Everywhere

Identify uses of technology

NAME _____

The Peanut Gallery

If you visit Georgia, you're likely to see a peanut farm. A scientist named George Washington Carver, who lived from 1861 to 1943, discovered more than 300 uses for peanuts. Some of those uses are listed below. See if you can "discover" them in the word find! Words go up, down, forward, and backward. When you're done, write the leftover letters in the order you find them on the blanks. They'll answer this riddle: What do you call a peanut that plays on a baseball team?

A peanut ____ ____ ____ ____ ____ ____

One way to start a word find is to look for the longest word first. Then look for the second longest word, and so on.

```
F  A  B  R  I  C  B  S
U  K  D  Y  E  E  A  H
E  N  T  T  U  R  R  A
L  I  N  O  L  E  U  M
T  L  I  O  G  A  O  P
S  O  A  P  E  L  L  O
P  A  P  E  R  R  F  O
```

Word List
SOAP
OIL
INK
PAINT
DYE
CEREAL
SHAMPOO
LINOLEUM
FABRIC
GLUE
FLOUR
FUEL
PAPER

Around the House: Look at different boxes and cans of food in your kitchen. Can you find any that list peanuts or peanut oil as an ingredient? Corn is also used in many products. See how often you can find corn, corn syrup, and corn oil in ingredient lists.

Grades 3 & 4

Chow Choice

Here, There, Everywhere
Add and subtract money

You're on the road again. You stop at a truck stop to buy lunch and gas. You have exactly $15.00 to spend. Out of that $15.00 you need to buy:

| gas | a fruit | a drink |
| a sandwich | a snack | |

The trick is—you must spend all your money, so you fill up your car first. It costs $6.70. Now you must spend the rest of your $15.00 on lunch. What foods can you buy? Add and subtract items on the lunch menu to find out.

> If you're a little confused, start by subtracting the money spent on gas ($6.70) from the total ($15.00). That will tell you how much you have left to spend on food.

> Then begin adding up different combinations of sandwiches, fruits, snacks, and drinks. You will eventually find a combination that is equal to the amount of money you have left.

MENU

Sandwiches

Avocado $5.25

Cheese $4.50

Tuna $5.00

Turkey $5.50

Snacks

Cookies $1.50

Pistachio Pie $2.00

Chocolate Bar $2.50

Drinks

Apple juice $1.30

Soda $1.25

Milk $1.15

Fruit

Apple . . . . $.55

Banana . . . . $.50

Around the House: Try making up challenges like this one for your family and friends. Give each person a budget and a catalog. Have them figure out what they can buy from the catalog that is within their budget.

Grades 3 & 4

Here, There, Everywhere

Find perimeter

NAME _____

Pony Power

> To figure out the perimeter of each pen, just add the lengths of all of the sides together. This sum is the *perimeter*.

> Well, you sure didn't horse around with that one! Good work. Now cut out this puzzle piece and glue or tape it to the frame on page 64.

Jason and Jessica Hoedown are visiting Chincoteague, Virginia. They are busy rounding up wild ponies because it is Pony Penning Day. Their job is to put the ponies into pens. There's just one problem: not all of the pens are big enough. Can you help them find the pens they can put ponies in? Figure out the perimeter of each pen. Write the result inside it. If the perimeter is less than 50 feet, it can't be used—it's just too small for the ponies to have room to run around. Cross it out!

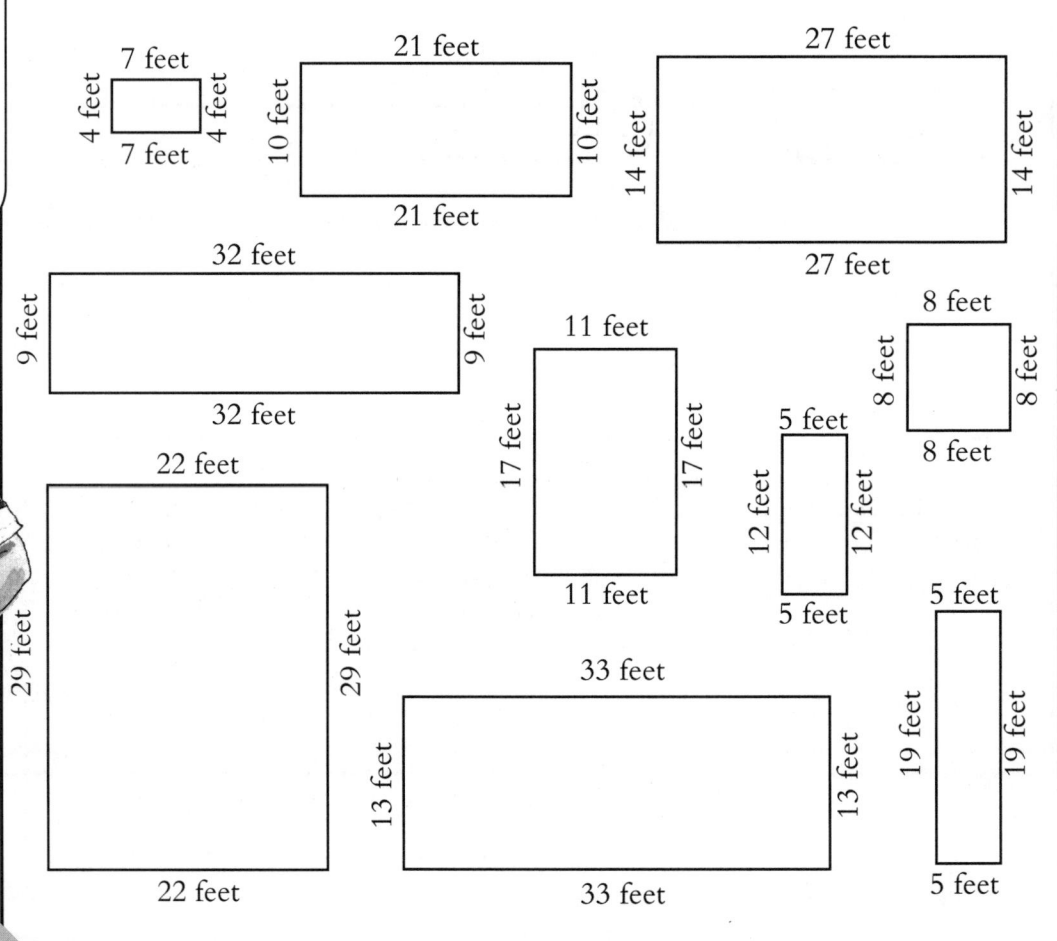

52

Grades 3 & 4

NAME _____

Great Times in D.C.

Here, There, Everywhere
Tell time to the minute

It's 9 A.M., and Sam Adams is thrilled to be in Washington, D.C. He wants to see it all—but he's got a plane to catch at 7:10 P.M. Which bus tours can he take before he has to leave? Help him figure out what time each bus leaves and returns. First, read the clocks. Then write the time that each clock says in the blank next to it. Cross out the tours he won't be able to take—without missing his plane!

A clock's little hand points to the hours. The big hand points to the minutes. Each little mark on the clock equals one minute.

So this clock says 10:09.

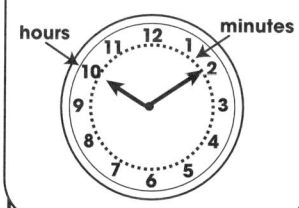

CAPITOL
Leaving Returning
_____ A.M. _____ P.M.

NATIONAL ZOO
Leaving Returning
_____ P.M. _____ P.M.

WASHINGTON MONUMENT
Leaving Returning
_____ P.M. _____ P.M.

NATIONAL AIR + SPACE MUSEUM
Leaving Returning
_____ P.M. _____ P.M.

SMITHSONIAN
Leaving Returning
_____ P.M. _____ P.M.

WHITE HOUSE
Leaving Returning
_____ P.M. _____ P.M.

Grades 3 & 4
53

Here, There, Everywhere

Identify elements of a biography

NAME _____

That's the Life

A biography is the story of a person's life. A good biography will leave you feeling as if you know the person—at least a little bit. Read the minibiography on this page. Answer the questions below.

It's a good idea to read the story straight through before reading the questions. Then you can go back and read it again to find the answers.

The Wandering Farmer

Johnny Appleseed's real name was John Chapman. Very little is known about his early life. He was born in Massachusetts in 1774. When he was almost 25, he started traveling across Ohio, Indiana, and Illinois. And that's how he spent the rest of his life—giving out seeds and taking care of the groves of apple trees he had planted. Some say that he would not cut branches from his trees because he thought it was mean to do such a thing. He loved nature with all his heart. One story tells how he set a wolf free from a trap, and it followed him around like a dog. He died in 1845, but stories about this barefoot, bearded traveler are still told today.

Who is the biography about? _____

When was he born? _____

When did he die? _____

Where did he live or spend most of his life? _____

What is he known for? That is, why is he famous? _____

_____

What kind of a person do you think he was? Why? _____

What did he look like? _____

What story about him interests you the most? _____

Would you like to find more information about this person in a longer biography? _____

Grades 3 & 4

NAME_____

Something Fishy

Marina Clambake is visiting the National Aquarium in Baltimore, Maryland. She is keeping a checklist of the fish she sees there. Be a sharp-eyed fish watcher and help her out. How many fish can you find that look exactly like these fish in the chart below? Circle the fish as you find them. Then write the total in the blank next to each fish in the chart.

Sightseeing and Souvenirs
Compare and contrast

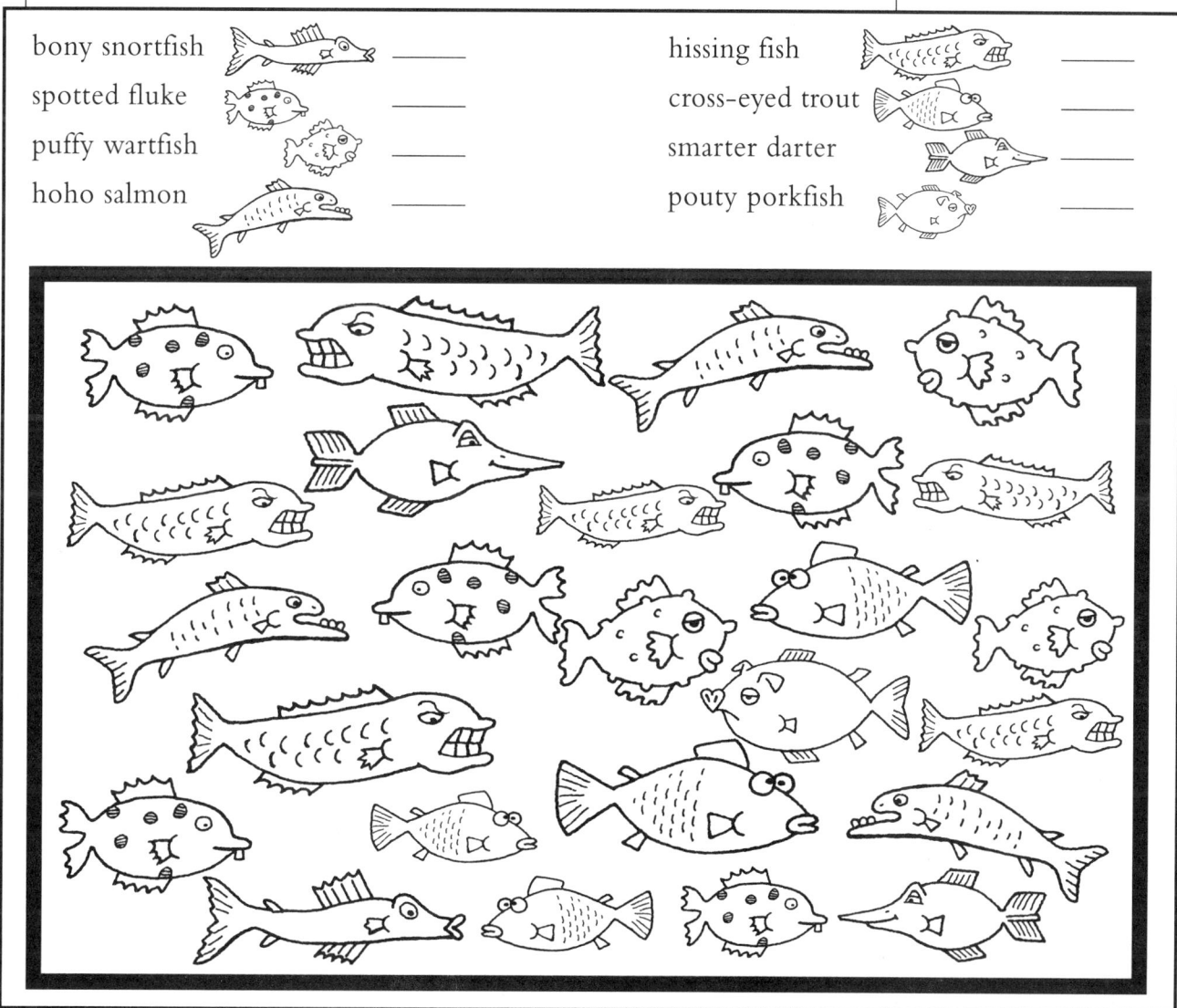

Grades 3 & 4

55

Sightseeing and Souvenirs

Round, then estimate addition and subtraction

NAME _____

Ride On!

Reilly Wildride visited an amusement park on the New Jersey shore. The rides there were so exciting that he was left almost speechless! He's trying to describe the rides—but he's at a loss for adjectives. Help him out by filling in the missing adjectives in his story. We've suggested a few adjectives in the word box below. But use your own if you can.

> An *adjective* is a word that describes a noun or pronoun. *Super, green, scary, freckled,* and *freaky* are all adjectives!

I spent the day at Rumbling Acres on the Jersey shore. Wow! What a day! First I rode on a roller-coaster called _____ Thunderbolt. It whipped me in circles and even upside down. Then I rode the teacup ride. I picked a _____ teacup. Next I hopped into a dodge-'em car. My car was _____ and _____ . I slammed into a _____ car driven by a _____ kid really hard! After that, I leaped onto the merry-go-round. I picked a _____ horse. Around and around we went.

furious
huge
wild
speedy
enormous
ridiculous
weird
scrumptious

This made me hungry, so I bought a mile-long hotdog, which was _____ , and a _____ glass of lemonade. It seemed like a good time to ride another roller coaster. This time I chose _____ Mind-Twister, a _____ ride. There's no floor in the car, and your feet just dangle in space! It zoomed up and down a zillion times. After I got off, I felt _____ . When my head stopped spinning, I bought a _____ ice cream cone with _____ sprinkles.

Next I played some games. They were pretty _____ . The only one I liked was a game in which you threw hoops over some stuffed animals. I won a _____ dinosaur and a _____ hat. I gave the dinosaur to my _____ brother. The day ended with _____ fireworks. Boy, was I _____ by the time we got to the car!

Larger than Life

Sightseeing and Souvenirs

Round, then estimate addition and subtraction

Libby Ellis is visiting the Statue of Liberty. She's trying to make sense of all the amazing facts and figures about the statue, so she wants to round off the different measurements to the nearest ten. Help her round them off and then figure out the word problems below. One measurement is done.

> One foot equals 12 inches. So if your measurement includes an extra few inches, round it down to the nearest foot. Round a measurement 6 inches or over up to the nearest foot. Then you can round that number to the nearest ten.

Measurements:

Total height: 305 feet, 6 inches
Statue, not including pedestal: 151 feet, 1 inch
Statue's right arm: 42 feet
Statue's hand: 16 feet, 5 inches
Statue's finger: 8 inches
Statue's nose: 4 feet, 6 inches
Tablet: 23 feet, 7 inches long
Statue's head: 28 feet from neck to points of crown

1. How much longer is the statue's head than her tablet?
   Original problem: 28 feet (statue's head length) – 23 feet, 7 inches (tablet length)
   Using rounded numbers: **30 feet – 24 feet = 6 feet**
   The head is about **6 feet** longer than the tablet.

2. About how tall is the pedestal?
   Original problem: 305 feet, 6 inches (height of whole statue) – 151 feet, 1 inch (height of statue, not including pedestal) =
   Using rounded numbers: _____
   The pedestal is about _____ tall.

3. How long is the statue's arm not including the hand?
   Original problem: 42 feet (length of arm) – 16 feet, 5 inches (length of hand)
   Using rounded numbers: _____
   Not including the hand, the arm is about _____ long.

Grades 3 & 4

Sightseeing and Souvenirs

Identify life cycle of animals

NAME _____

Rhode Island Ready

While visiting Rhode Island, Henrietta Leghorn learned about its state bird—the Rhode Island Red. She decided to start her own chicken farm and raise Rhode Island Reds. But first she must learn as much as she can about the life cycle of this animal. Help her out by numbering these 8 pictures so that she can look at them in the right order. To help you get started, we put a "1" on the picture that should come first.

Most animals go through a predictable cycle of changes like these.
If you're not sure about the order of events in the life of a chicken, use an encyclopedia or reference book from your library.

58

Grades 3 & 4

Beantown

Paula Revere is visiting Boston, the capital city of Massachusetts. Boston is a very old city. Paula wants to find out about its history and when some of its famous buildings were constructed, but someone has erased almost everything from the time line! Help her out by putting the events listed in the chart onto the time line.

A *time line* is a kind of number line. You put marks along it at different points to show when things happened.

The big marks on this time line mark off every 20 years. The point halfway between two big marks is a ten-year mark.

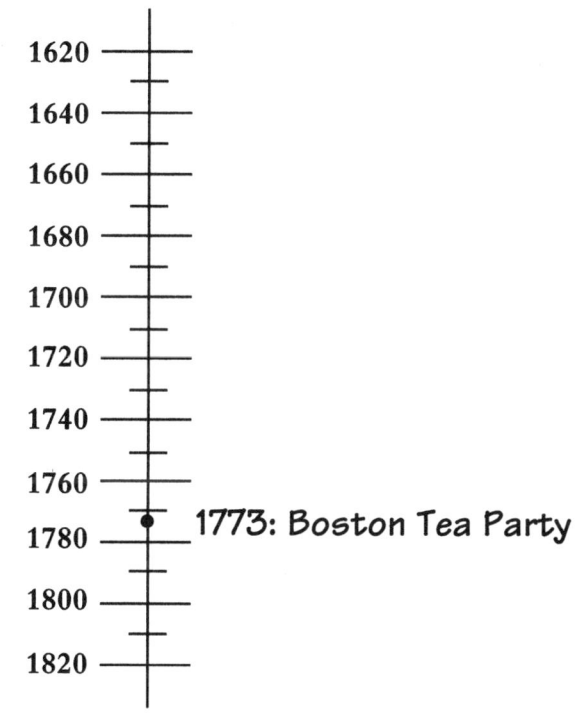

1773: Boston Tea Party

1712: Old Corner Bookstore built	1742: Faneuil Hall built
1634: Boston Common opened	1806: African Meeting House built
1748: Old State House built	1770: Boston Massacre
1680: Paul Revere house built	1630: Boston declared a town
1773: Boston Tea Party	1723: Old North Church built
1798: "Constitution" ship launched	

Sightseeing and Souvenirs
Draw a time line

Sightseeing and Souvenirs
Write a review

NAME _____

Write a Review

Read the sample hotel review written here. Then think of a place you have visited, slept in, or eaten in. On another piece of paper, write a review of the place. Use our questions to help you think of what to write.

Renee's Review

I stayed at a new hotel called The Giant Eggplant during the July 4 weekend. This hotel is shaped like an eggplant! My room was cozy, with a nice view of the beach. The bed was bouncy, but not too squishy. I slept like a log! The air conditioning was too cold, and I could not figure out how to turn it down. There is also a restaurant in the hotel. It serves vegetarian meals. At first, I was worried. I don't like chunks of raw carrots mixed with brown rice. Then I got my meal—and it was great! I had a veggie burger with fresh tomatoes and crisp lettuce. The french fries were curly and salted perfectly. The meal came with a bright, pink fruit drink that was not too sweet, not too sour—just right! The service could have been better, though. I was ignored for about 10 minutes after sitting down. But it's still a new place, so I'll give it another try for sure.

Here are the questions to help you begin thinking.
What is the name of the place you visited?
When did you visit?
Would you tell your friends to go there? Why?
What is the best thing about this place?
What is the worst thing about this place?
How would you change the place to make it better?

Around the House: Write a review of a book you have read or a TV show you watch.

You've earned a rave review for this page! Now cut out the puzzle piece and glue or tape it on page 64.

NAME_____

Roots and Leaves

Sightseeing and Souvenirs

Identify prefixes and suffixes

Roz Berry, plant scientist, is visiting New England, an area of the country famous for its colorful fall trees. She loves to rake, so she wants to rake these leaves into two piles: One pile should contain only leaves with words that contain prefixes. The other pile should contain only leaves with words that contain suffixes. Help Roz out. Color the leaves for the prefixes pile orange. Color the leaves for the suffixes pile yellow.

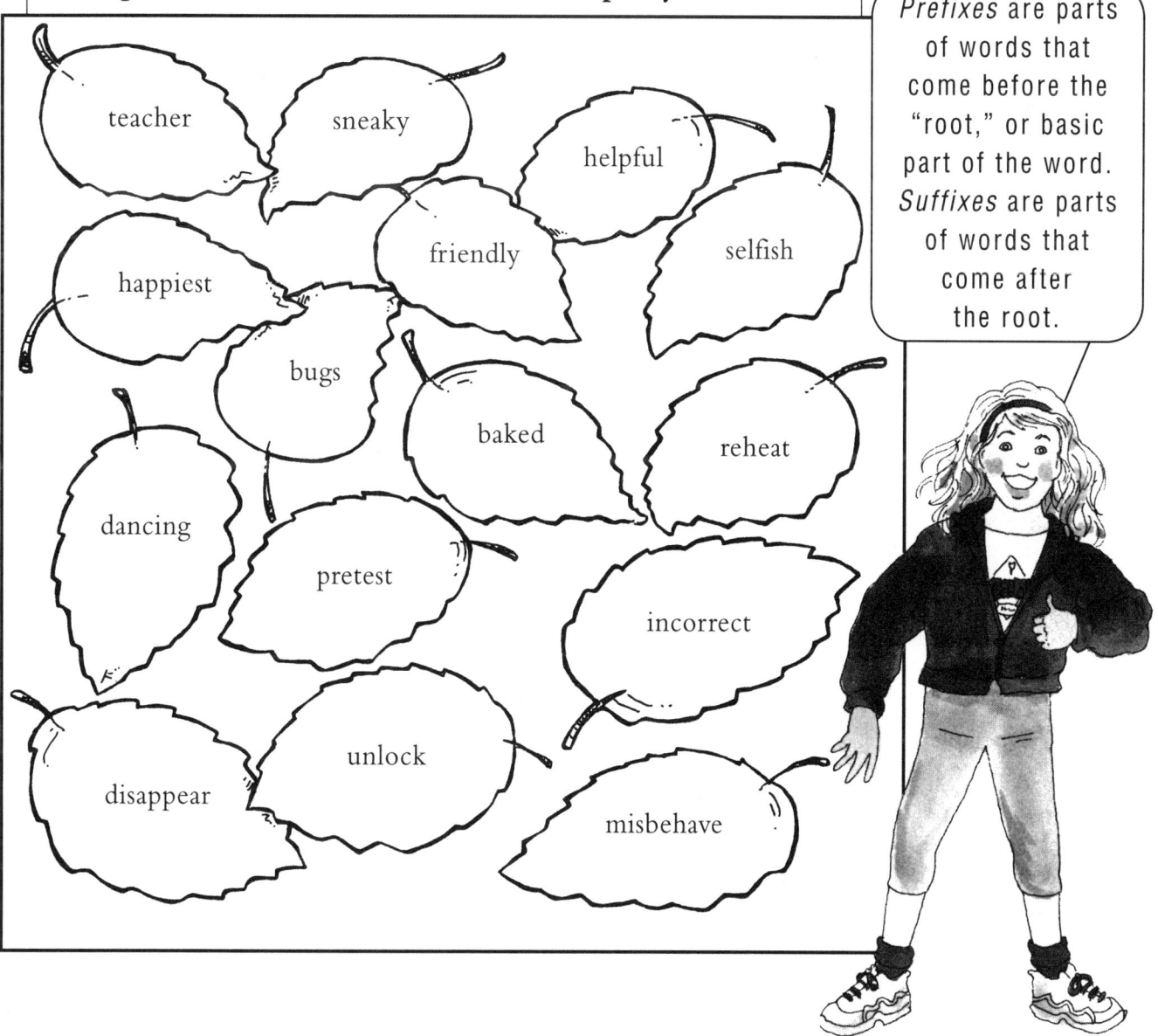

Prefixes are parts of words that come before the "root," or basic part of the word. *Suffixes* are parts of words that come after the root.

Leaves: teacher, sneaky, helpful, happiest, friendly, selfish, bugs, baked, reheat, dancing, pretest, incorrect, disappear, unlock, misbehave

Grades 3 & 4

Sightseeing and Souvenirs

Use basic abbreviations

NAME _____

Gee, Thanks!

Roger Dodger is back from his vacation across the U.S.A. He's brought home T-shirts and matching caps to give to all his friends. The shirts have names of states on them. The caps have the abbreviations for the states on them. But the shirts and caps have gotten all mixed up. Draw a line from each state name to its abbreviation.

Some abbreviations are easy to spot—but others are tricky! Some states start with the same letter or letters. So the abbreviations use letters from any part of the word—not just the beginning!

62

Grades 3 & 4

NAME_____

Good Buy!

Sightseeing and Souvenirs
Multiply money

You're buying souvenirs to bring home to your friends. You want to know how much the items cost. The store owner, however, has made math problems out of the prices! You have to do two things:

Coin List
1 penny = 1 cent
1 nickel = 5 cents
1 dime = 10 cents
1 quarter = 25 cents

1. Multiply to figure out the 2 parts of the price.
2. Add the 2 answers to get the total price.
We did one for you to get you started.

Cut out this last puzzle piece to finish the picture on page 64! Glue or tape it in the frame.

1.

5 dimes + 3 nickels
First math problem: 5 x __10__ = __50¢__
Second math problem: 3 x __5__ = __15¢__
Add the results! This item costs __65¢__

2.

9 nickels + 8 pennies
First math problem: ___ x ___ = ___
Second math problem: ___ x ___ = ___
Add the results! This item costs _____

3.

2 quarters + 3 dimes
First math problem: ___ x ___ = ___
Second math problem: ___ x ___ = ___
Add the results! This item costs _____

4.

3 quarters + 2 nickels
First math problem: ___ x ___ = ___
Second math problem: ___ x ___ = ___
Add the results! This item costs _____

Puzzle

Here's where you glue or paste the puzzle pieces you cut out. When you put them all in place, you'll see your secret message.

Answers

Page 1
Gloria can travel to Brazil and India.

Page 2
Answers will vary.

Page 3
bathing suit, beach ball, beach bucket, beach towel, boat, cap, inflatable shark, jeans, juice, sandals, sandwiches, shirts, shorts, shovel, sneakers, socks, sunglasses, sunscreen, sweater, umbrella

Page 4
Sample answer: bunch of shirts, two pairs of jeans, salami, hiking shoes, laptop computer, dinosaur, binoculars, camera, guitar, box of cookies

Page 5
1. boat
2. jet
3. small plane
4. jeep
5. bicycle
6. helicopter
7. train
8. horse

Page 6–7
Mountains: Toe, Tootle, Teacozy, Tired Elk
Lakes: Oodle, Oops
Parks: Aching Back, Antsinpants, Angrybear
Capitals: Double
Wetlands: Martian Swamp, Mooskunk
Campgrounds: Aching Feet, Ambush,
Racetracks: Pony Acres
Riddle answer: TOAD MAP

Matching key:

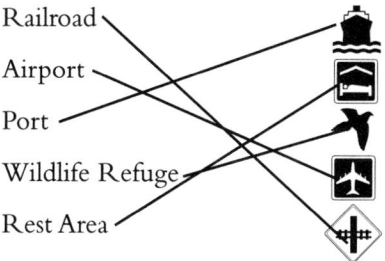

Page 8
The 20 mistakes are as follows:
1. Lake Erie is labeled as Superior.
2. Lake Superior is labeled as Erie.
3. South Carolina is labeled as North Carolina.
4. North Carolina is labeled as South Carolina.
5. Mississippi is spelled Mississippi.
6. Iowa has Ohio's name on it.
7. Ohio has Iowa's name on it.
8. Rhode Island has been left off the map.
9. West Dakota should be South Dakota.
10. Virginia should just be Virginia, not East Virginia.
11. There is no state called Old Mexico.
12. The Arizona River should be the Colorado River.
13. The Great Salt Lake is in Utah, not Wyoming.
14. The Stony Mountains are really the Rocky Mountains.
15. Oregon has Washington's name on it.
16. Washington has Oregon's name on it.
17. Lake Wisconisin should be Lake Michigan.
18. Washington, D.C. is not in Maine.
19. Kansas has Arkansas's name on it.
20. Arkansas has Kansas's name on it.

Page 9
1. Imelda took off from Idaho.
2. She landed in Arizona.
3. After eating lunch, she flew to New Mexico.
4. She then flew to Colorado.
5. Then she flew to Montana.
6. She was in South Dakota.
7. Finally, she landed in Utah.

Page 10

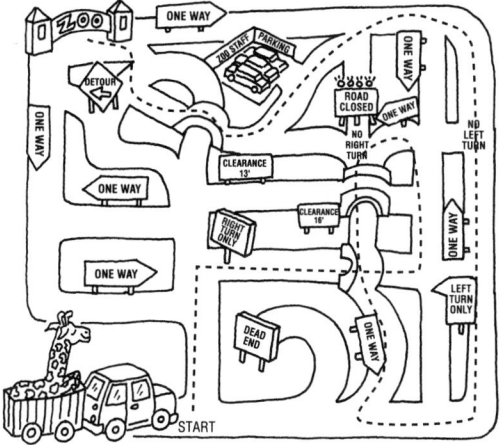

Grades 3 & 4

Page 11

Hidden word: ALOHA

Page 12
Answers will vary.
Possible answers include:
Luggage—bags, suitcases, trunks, equipment
Car—auto, automobile, van
Hotel—motel, inn, lodge, resort
Restaurant—cafe, diner, deli
Beach—shore, seashore, seaside, ocean, coast
Boat—sailboat, vessel, craft, ship
Pictures—photos, photographs, snapshots
Fun—interesting, exciting, entertaining

Page 13
Jellyfish, seashore, catfish, dogsled, dogfish, catbird, seabird, butterfly, buttercup, butterfish, jellybean, seaweed, dragonfly, dragonfish, eyeball, football, baseball, basketball, butterball

Pages 14–15
1. 11:13 A.M.
2. 2:01 P.M.
3. 3:13 P.M.
4. Saturday at 12:55 A.M.
5. 3:12 A.M.
6. 4:11 A.M.
7. 6:31 P.M.
8. 5:37 P.M.
9. 4:55 P.M.

Riddle answer: Because they're SHELLFISH!

Page 16

Page 17
The miner with $\frac{1}{2}$ on his shirt found the most gold. Five of the gold nuggets in his pile contain equivalent fractions: $\frac{2}{4}, \frac{3}{6}, \frac{4}{8}, \frac{5}{10}, \frac{6}{12}$. The $\frac{1}{4}$ miner found three nuggets: $\frac{2}{8}, \frac{3}{12}, \frac{4}{16}$. The $\frac{1}{3}$ miner found three nuggets: $\frac{2}{6}, \frac{3}{9}, \frac{4}{12}$.

Page 18
1. 14 x 9 = 126
2. 8 x 15 = 120
3. 7 x 18 = 126
4. 6 x 22 = 132
5.
6. 59 x 2 = 118
7. 9 x 13 = 117
8. 44 x 3 = 132
9. 5 x 23 = 115

Number 9 is coolest.

Page 19
1. b
2. c
3. a
4. b
5. a
6. c
7. a
8. b

Page 20
Didi's dinosaur is a Torvosaurus.

Page 21
1. and
2. or
3. yet
4. but
5. so

Page 22
Answers will vary.

Page 23
Heather's motel is in Lower Upsville. On the first day, she drove 22 miles. On the second day, she drove 30 miles. On the third day, she racked up 10 miles.

Page 24

Page 25

I'm George Washington, the first president of the United States. I served from 1789 to 1797. By the way, that story about how I cut down a cherry tree isn't really true!

I'm Thomas Jefferson. I was president number three. When I bought a large chunk of land, it became known as the Louisiana Purchase. I had a pet mockingbird that would sit on my shoulder!

I'm Theodore Roosevelt, president number twenty-six. I am famous for saying "speak softly and carry a big stick." I was the first president to ride in a plane.

I'm Abraham Lincoln, the sixteenth president. I led the nation during the Civil War. A little girl gave me the suggestion to grow a beard! I gave a speech that set all slaves free. Sad to say, I was shot and killed.

Page 26

378 ÷ 2 = 189
644 ÷ 4 = 161
910 ÷ 7 = 130
928 ÷ 8 = 116
999 ÷ 9 = 111
459 ÷ 3 = 153
984 ÷ 6 = 164
713 ÷ 1 = 713
710 ÷ 5 = 142

Riddle answer: IT WOULD BECOME A PINK CARNATION!

Page 27

Kicking Horse, MT/Deadhorse, AK
Sour Lake, TX/Sweetwater, TN
Hot Coffee, MS/Coldwater, MO
Normal, IL/Peculiar, MO
Evening Star, AR/Morning Sun, AR
Nice, CA/Savage, MT
Summersville, MT/Winterville, NC
Black Horse, OH/White Horse, NM
Sunrise, FL/Sunset, AR
Advance, NC/Retreat, GA
Big Rock, VA/Little Rock, AR
Painesville, OH/Pleasureville, PA
Cold Springs, KY/Boiling Springs, PA
Westhampton, NY/Easthampton, MA
Warfield, KY/Peace Valley, MO
High Point, MO/Lowpoint, IL

Page 28–29

1. Beaver City 1-I, Beaver Crossing 7-G
2. Cook 10-H
3. Hazard 3-F
4. Wakefield 8-B
5. Poole 3-F
6. Roseland 4-H, Primrose 5-E
7. Red Cloud 4-I
8. Broken Arrow 1-E
9. Superior 5-I
10. Friend 7-G
11. Page 4-B
12. Bassett 2-B
13. Plainview 6-B

Page 30

Answers will vary.

Page 31

Answers will vary.

Page 32–33

1. about 8 Minnies
2. shortest: Big Tex; tallest: CN Tower
3. 1,763 feet
4. about 12 models of Big Tex
5. 15 feet
6. the redwood, by 90 feet
7. 235 feet
8. 108 feet
9. 3 Space Needles
10. about 18 Minnies
11. 254 feet
12. answers will vary

Page 34

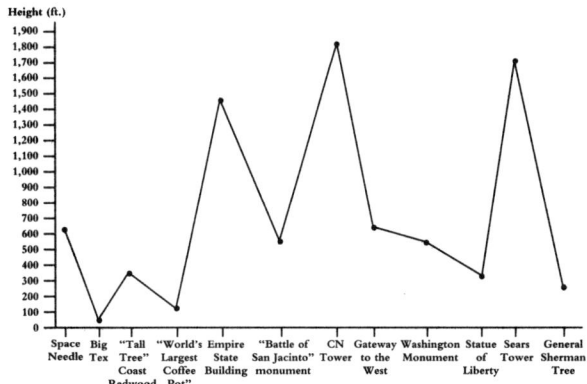

Page 35

Answers will vary.

Page 36
Super Bran Broncobits is Nick's favorite cereal.

Page 37
Answers will vary.

Page 38–39
Game will vary.

Page 40
A. 200; 14 hours
B. 200; 350 squirts
C. 300; 26 pounds
D. 700; 100 pounds
E. 700; 100,000,000
F. 700; 1,500 pounds
G. 500; 10 gallons

Page 41
Answers will vary.

Page 42
1. What did Tennessee? The same thing that Arkansas!
2. What did Bob say when he figured out his Texas? "Gee, Iowa lot of money!"
3. Do you know how to get to the North Pole? Neither do I, but Alaska reindeer if I see one!
4. What did Delaware to the party? She wore her New Jersey!
5. What do you buy if you're just a little thirsty? A Minnesota.
6. Is Ore still here? No, Oregon.
7. A gardener had a helper named Ida. But Ida simply would not use a rake. What should the gardener do? Let Idaho and do the raking himself!
8. What did the teacher call Mr. Sippi's wife? Mississippi
9. What state is best for cars? Rhode Island
10. Where should you take your laundry? Washington

Page 43
1. The bear ate the most pizza. It gobbled up 9 slices.
2. The crow ate the least pizza. It ate only 3 slices.
3. The humans were left with just 7 slices: 3 pepperoni, 1 anchovy, 1 pepper, and 2 sprout-and-mushroom.

Page 44

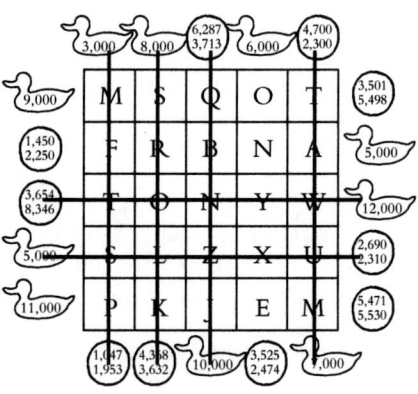

If you racked up 45,000 points, you win a big stuffed rhino.
Riddle answer: One. After that, the bathtub isn't empty anymore!

Page 45
Answers will vary.

Page 46

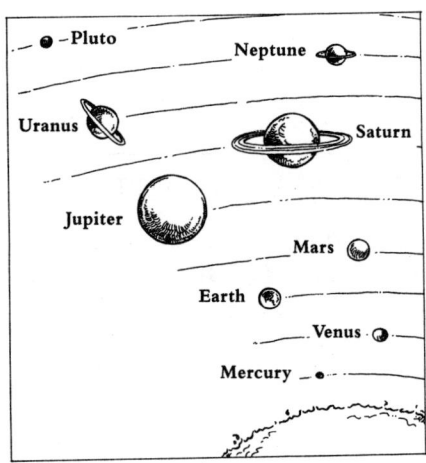

Pages 47
Dear, ate, tail, eight, piece, deer, bear, hole, bare, hear, tale, peace, whole, here

Page 48
An alligator keep growing thoughout its life. F
It's better to be a warm-blooded animal than a cold-blooded one. O
An alligator's lower teeth are hidden inside its mouth when it shuts its jaws. F
An alligator grows new teeth to replace old ones all its life. F
Alligators are quite beautiful. O
An alligator uses its tail to swim. F
Alligators don't have any feelings. O
Alligators build nests out of leaves, branches, and mud piled into a heap. F

The alligator is the most interesting animal in America. O

A mother alligator may help her babies break out of their shells and even hold the little ones in her mouth for safety. F

An alligator can grow to be 20 feet long. F

Alligators are frightening animals. O

Page 49
Answers will vary.

Page 50

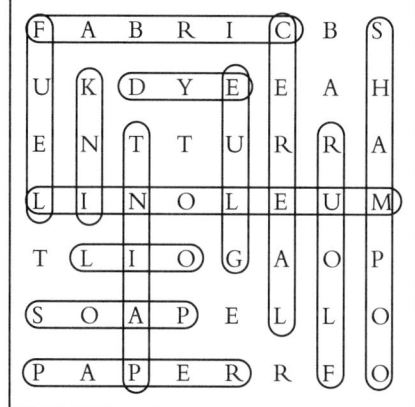

Riddle answer: A peanut BATTER.

Page 51
You can buy a cheese sandwich, a banana, apple juice, and pistachio pie OR a tuna sandwich, a banana, apple juice, and cookies. Each combination adds up to $8.30, and $8.30 + $6.70 = $15.00.

Page 52

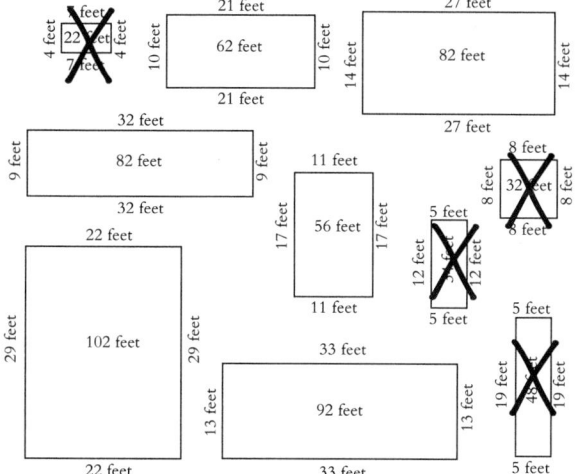

Page 53
Capitol: 9:15, 11:05
National Zoo: 2:39, 8:27
Washington Monument: 2:53, 8:45
National Air and Space Museum: 3:17, 9:08
Smithsonian: 2:53, 8:45
White House: 3:53, 8:45
All tours should be crossed out because they return too late for Sam to catch his plane.

Page 54
Johnny Appleseed/John Chapman; born in 1774; died in 1845; lived in Massachusetts; traveled across Ohio, Indiana, and Illinois; rest of answers will vary.

Page 55
There is 1 bony snortfish.
There are 5 spotted fluke.
There are 3 puffy wartfish.
There are 3 hoho salmon.
There are 6 hissing fish.
There are 4 cross-eyed trout.
There are 2 smarter darter.
There is 1 pouty porkfish.

Page 56
Answers will vary.

Page 57
2. Original problem: 305 feet, 6 inches (height of whole statue) − 151 feet, 1 inch (height of statue, not including pedestal) =
   Using rounded numbers: 310 feet − 150 feet = 160 feet.
   The pedestal is about 160 feet tall.

3. Original problem: 42 feet (length of arm) − 16 feet, 5 inches (length of hand) =
   Using rounded numbers: 40 feet − 20 feet = 20 feet.
   Not including the hand, the arm is about 20 feet long.

Page 58
1. Hen scraping ground with leg and using beak to settle hay and stuff around her to make a nest.
2. Hen standing over nest with 4 eggs in it.
3. Closeup on 4 eggs, one is starting to have cracks in it.
4. Same closeup, but now chick is halfway out of egg.
5. Same scene, but now chick is completely out of egg, and is lying there all wet and floppy.
6. Same scene, now chick is standing and is completely dry, and there is a crack beginning in another egg.
7. All 4 chicks are hatched out, dry, eggshells lying around empty.
8. Mother hen and chicks are away from nest, searching for food.

Page 59

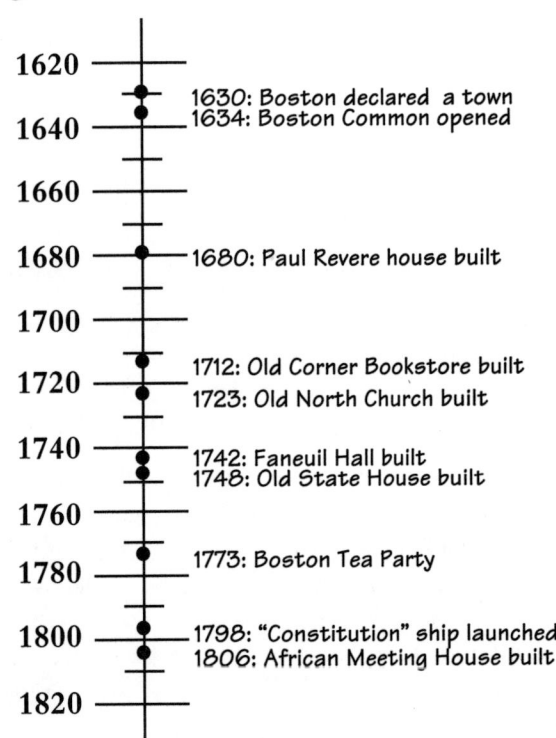

Page 62

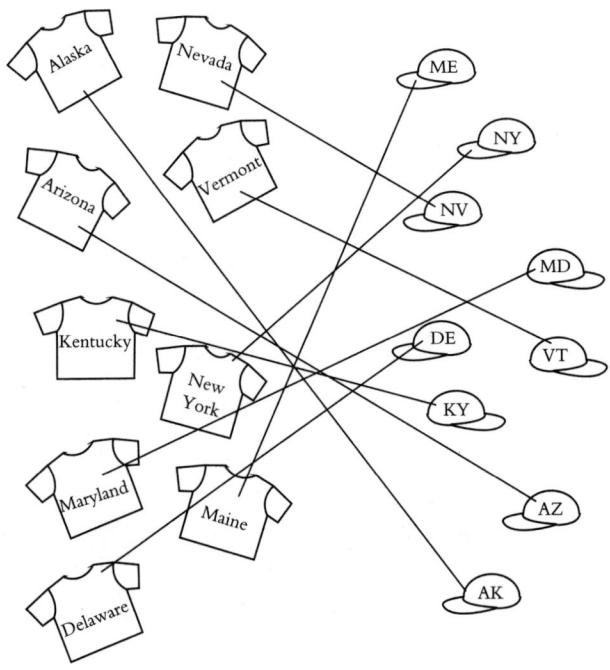

Page 63
2. 9 x 5 = 45
    8 x 1 = 8
    45 + 8 = 53, so this item costs 53¢.

3. 2 x 25 = 50
    3 x 10 = 30
    50 + 30 = 80, so this item costs 80¢.

4. 3 x 25 = 75
    2 x 5 = 10
    75 + 10 = 85, so this item costs 85¢.

Page 60
Answers will vary.

Page 61
Orange leaves: reheat, pretest, incorrect, unlock, disappear, misbehave
Yellow leaves: teacher, sneaky, helpful, selfish, friendly, happiest, bugs, baked, dancing

How Do You Foster Your Child's Interest in Learning?

In preparing this series, we surveyed scores of parents on this key question. Here are some of the best suggestions:

- Take weekly trips to the library to take out books, and attend special library events.

- Have lots of books around the house, especially on topics of specific interest to children.

- Read out loud nightly.

- Take turns reading to each other.

- Subscribe to age-appropriate magazines.

- Point out articles of interest in the newspaper or a magazine.

- Tell each other stories.

- Encourage children to write journal entries and short stories.

- Ask them to write letters and make cards for special occasions.

- Discuss all the things you do together.

- Limit TV time.

- Watch selected programs on TV together, like learning/educational channels.

- Provide project workbooks purchased at teacher supply stores.

- Supply lots of arts and crafts materials and encourage children to be creative.

- Encourage children to express themselves in a variety of ways.

- Take science and nature walks.

- Teach children to play challenging games such as chess.

- Provide educational board games.

- Supply lots of educational and recreational computer games.

- Discuss what children are learning and doing on a daily basis.

- Invite classmates and other friends over to your house for team homework assignments.

- Keep the learning experiences fun for children.

- Help children with their homework and class assignments.

- Take trips to museums and museum classes.

- Visits cities of historical interest.

- Takes trips to the ocean and other fun outdoor locations (fishing at lakes, mountain hikes).

Grades 3 & 4

- Visit the aquarium and zoo.
- Cook, bake, and measure ingredients.
- Encourage children to participate in sports.
- Listen to music, attend concerts, and encourage children to take music lessons.
- Be positive about books, trips, and other daily experiences.
- Take family walks.
- Let children be part of the family decision-making process.
- Sit down together to eat and talk.
- Give a lot of praise and positive reinforcement for your child's efforts.
- Review child's homework that has been returned by the teacher.
- Encourage children to use resources such as the dictionary, encyclopedia, thesaurus, and atlas.
- Plant a vegetable garden outdoors or in pots in your kitchen.
- Make each child in your family feel he or she is special.
- Don't allow children to give up, especially when it comes to learning and dealing with challenges.
- Instill a love of language; it will expose your child to a richer thought bank.
- Tell your children stories that share, not necessarily teach a lesson.
- Communicate your personal processes with your children.
- Don't talk about what your child did not do. Put more interest on what your child did do. Accept where your child is at, and praise his or her efforts.
- Express an interest in children's activities and schoolwork.
- Limit TV viewing time at home and foster good viewing habits.
- Work on enlarging children's vocabulary.
- Emphasize learning accomplishments, no matter how small.
- Go at their own pace; People learn at different rates.
- Challenge children to take risks.
- Encourage them to do their best, not be the best.